THE NECESSARY ANGEL

SUNY Series, Intersections:
Philosophy and Critical Theory

Rodolphe Gasché and Mark C. Taylor, Editors

THE NECESSARY ANGEL

MASSIMO CACCIARI

TRANSLATED BY
MIGUEL E. VATTER

STATE UNIVERSITY OF NEW YORK PRESS

Published by
State University of New York Press, Albany

For information, address State University of New York
Press, State University Plaza, Albany, N.Y., 12246

Production by Diane Ganeles
Marketing by Fran Keneston

Library of Congress Cataloging-in-Publication Data

Cacciari, Massimo,
    [Angelo necessario. English]
    The necessary angel / Massimo Cacciari ; translated by Miguel E.
Vatter.
        p.   cm. — (SUNY series, intersections)
    Includes bibliographical references.
    ISBN 0–7914–2189–9 (alk. paper). — ISBN 0–7914–2190–2 (pbk. :
alk. paper)
    1. Angels—Comparative studies.   2. Angel—History of doctrines.
3. Angels in art.   4. Angels in literature.   I. Title.   II. Series:
Intersections (Albany, N.Y.)
BL477.C3313   1994
291.2'15—dc20   93–50119
                                                                    CIP

10 9 8 7 6 5 4 3 2 1

CONTENTS

Preface to the French Edition/vii

Preface to the English Edition/viii

Translator's Note/ix

1. Since the Days of Tobias/1

2. Angel and Demon/15

3. The Problem of Representation/39

4. Zodiacs/55

5. Apokatastasis/67

6. Birds of the Soul/83

Notes/95

PREFACE
TO THE FRENCH EDITION (1988)

This book accompanies me already for a number of years, witness the title of the journal that I founded in 1964: *Angelus Novus*, but it was only after writing *Icone della Legge* (1985) that I felt the need to explain to myself the reasons for such an obstinate *philia*, the presence of this so patient friend.

In my quest for "these serene animals which approach God" (as Umberto Saba would have said), I have received the precious aid of Alessandro Fonti, who has collected and put at my disposal the complete series of drawings by Paul Klee on the figures of the Angel and the demon; Paolo Bettiolo, for the research and interpretation of the texts of the Judeo-Christian tradition; Nadia Fusini, whose translation of Wallace Stevens (from which I took the title of my book) constitutes a model reading and interpretation of a contemporary classic.

With respect to the Italian and German (Klagenfurt, 1987) editions, the French edition contains, primarily in the critical apparatus, a number of additions and insertions, and therefore is the definitive version of *L'Angelo necessario*.

Massimo Cacciari

PREFACE
TO THE ENGLISH EDITION

With respect to the French edition, the English edition is unchanged. Only some formal mistakes and some oversights have been corrected.

Massimo Cacciari

TRANSLATOR'S NOTE

Every translation comports a betrayal of the original that is occasioned by the very project of transmitting its sense, and as a condition for such transmission. In the crossing from one language to another, the translator makes innumerable decisions in which some aspects of the original are downplayed, disregarded, even sacrificed in the attempt to keep the vessel of the translation from foundering. Thus it is only fair that the translator should bring to attention what, in his opinion, has been lost during the journey.

The difficulty of Cacciari's prose is in great part due to the rhythm imposed by his practice of citation from foreign languages, the production of neologisms, the breaking up of words with the consequent release of polysemy. This writing, which, already in the original, at one time both calls for and repels translation, destroys the illusion of an organic language, and along with it the idea that fluidity is a *sigillum veri* of any translation. Cacciari's style is intrinsic to a philosophical project that views as problematic any claim made on behalf of discourse to the systematic comprehension, free of disruptions and holes, of that about which it speaks. But in translation one loses this very style which stages the text's oppositional complex of the continuous and the discontinuous, the disturbing spectacle of a language struggling against itself in the attempt to wrench from itself, or to bring into itself, semantic possibilities that would remain otherwise unavailable.

Avoiding the impossible task of a mimesis of such a style, this translator chose the alternative of exactitude in rendering the let-

ter of the text, trusting that if its spirit would survive the translation, it would do so through, and not against, its letter. In this
regard, Walter Benjamin's suggestion, that "if the sentence is the
wall before the language of the original, literalness is the
arcade," was taken to heart.

At the risk of burdening the text, but for the sake of that elusive quality of "readability", the following additions were made.
English translations were added for most foreign terms and
phrases when they first appear in the text; these are not intended to
replace the original but merely serve as pointers for the reader
unfamiliar with these languages. Notes were appended to explicate
word-play and hidden etymological references. Quotations were
rendered by standard English translations wherever possible,
otherwise the translations were made from the ones found in the
Italian original. The English editions of texts referred to in the
notes have also been provided.

Lastly, I wish to acknowledge those who have helped me carry
out the task: Mark C. Taylor and Rodolphe Gasché for accepting
and then encouraging the project, Carola Sautter for her editorial
support, Pierre Adler for his work on the Greek and Latin, Clifford
Ruprecht and Isabella Bertoletti for reading the various drafts and
making the necessary suggestions and corrections, each with a
trained eye to their respective mother-tongues, and Massimo
Cacciari for his "angelic" patience. To my parents, who always
somehow manage to make me bear lightly the immeasurable debt I
owe them, and to Rebecca Foster, who helps me find ways where
there seem to be none, I give thanks.

MIGUEL E. VATTER

THE NECESSARY ANGEL

I am the angel of reality,
Seen for a moment standing in the door.

I have neither ashen wing nor wear of ore
And live without a tepid aureole,

Or stars that follow me, not to attend,
But, of my being and its knowing, part.

I am one of you and being one of you
Is being and knowing what I am and know.

Yet I am the necessary angel of earth,
Since, in my sight, you see the earth again,

Cleared of its stiff and stubborn, man-locked set,
And, in my hearing, you hear its tragic drone

Rise liquidly in liquid lingerings,
Like watery words awash; like meanings said

By repetitions of half-meanings. Am I not,
Myself, only half of a figure of a sort,

A figure half seen for a moment, a man
Of the mind, an apparition apparelled in

Apparels of such lightest look that a turn
Of my shoulder and quickly, too quickly, I am gone?

Wallace Stevens, in *Angel Surrounded by Paysans*

1

SINCE
THE
DAYS
OF
TOBIAS

The dimension of the Angel is ou-topic. Its place is the Land-of-no-where, the mundus imaginalis,* whose fourth dimensio (axis) lies beyond the sphere that delimits the axes of the visible cosmos. No one could point to the path that leads there. Only the Angel, guardian of the divine Word, icon of the *ad*-verbum,[1] indispensable intermediary[2] of all the prophets[3] up to Muhammad, can undertake long journeys from the invisible No-where, from its Caelum Caeli (Heaven of Heaven), unchanging and eternal Domus (dwelling) and Civitas (city) of the Lord (St. Augustine, *Confessions*, XII, 11), toward the interior temple of man, enter his darkness, and help him recover his proper Orient. The Kabbalah teaches that Angels ascend and descend in the vast space of the Kingdom, so much so that they wonder whether their Lord dwells "above" or "below."[4] The nostalgia for the supreme Point that irrepressibly determines their movement, *is* itself the presence (the only conceivable presence) of that Point in the regions of the Kingdom. It gives itself in the intellectual light, in the matutinal knowledge whose archetype is the Cherub; it offers itself in the highest power to love of the Seraph, in the rotating spiritus (spirit) of the Ofannim: all indivisible aspects of the same, incessantly creative act of God,[5] of the advent that never ceases.

1

Thus Suhrawardi, in one of his great mystical tales, *Le bruise-ment des ailes de Gabriel*,[6] sees in Gabriel the dator formarum (giver of forms), Angel of knowledge ("Nunc scio vere, quia misit dominus angelum suum. Now I know truly that God has sent me His angel. When God sends His angel to the soul, she becomes truly knowing", Meister Eckhart, *Nunc scio vere*)[7], the hermeneut of the silence of the superior worlds, who restlessly passes between the visible and the invisible, witness and icon of the invisible.[8] The "God-nourishing" Silence (*Chaldean oracles*, fr. 16), in fact, can be gathered only by the *flower of the intellect* (ibid., fr. 1).[9] Unity with the Silence of the One in itself, Apex Mentis (summit of the mind), is attained by casting off every thing, exciting the highest faculty of the soul "beyond all entities . . . in the profound peace of every power" (Proclus, *In Platonis theologiam*, I, 3).[10] Likewise, the angel of Suhrawardi turns the soul toward that Apex and makes it move in harmony with its intelligible Sun. The angel essentially appears as Angelus interpres (mediator Angel), in accordance with the prophetic and, later, apocalyptic dimension indissolubly associated with its figure.[11] The forms of angelic communication differ in principle from those of sensible apprehension and sight. The Angel witnesses the mystery as mystery, transmits the invisible as invisi-ble, without "betraying" it to the senses.[12] The Angel most certainly is a mirror, but of "the divine purity of the stillness and mystery of God, as far as that may be" (Meister Eckhart, *Ecce mitto angelum meum*; Walshe trans., vol. 2, p. 37). It *figures* the living presence of the mystery[13]—but only for the gaze of pure *theory*. Theory does not correspond to spiritual realities as our seeing-knowing corre-sponds to sensible objects that are other with respect to our being. Man does not confront Truth as he confronts the world; in the world he "sees the sun without being sun; and he sees the heaven and the earth and all other things, but he is not these things" ("Gospel of Philip," 61:24–25);[14] to see something of this Land-of-no-where, though, he must transfigure himself into it. This is the profound Neoplatonic[15] inspiration of all mystical angelology which understands supreme theory as *henosis* (unification), as the disappearance of the distinction between subject and object.[16] While knowledge "is in a certain respect separated [from its object] by otherness" (Iamblichus, *De mysteriis Aegyptiorum*, I, 8),[17] the Angel e-ducates* to a vision in whose form object and subject become a "monad." The figure of the Angel is the sign that "we are surrounded by divine presence and from it we derive the fullness of our being."[18] The development and questioning of the fundamental "krisis" between knowledge and theōrein (contemplation) constitutes the most proper object of angelology: its annunciation does not concern the becoming visible of the invisible, the translating-betraying of the invisible in and for the visually perceptible, but the possibility for human beings to correspond to the invisible as such, to that Invisible which the Angel safeguards precisely in the instant in which it is communicated through its forms. The paradoxical character of this relation haunts and dominates angelology—this book follows its traces.[19]

The Angel transforms the gaze itself into a gaze of the no-where. To the mundus imaginalis figured by the Angel there must correspond the gaze of an imaginatio (a vision). The mysteries of the Angel can be intuited *sola mente* (only by the mind). The proliferation of angelic hypostases in the Gnostic and Christian-Gnostic traditions, just like in the developments of Neoplatonism and in Islam, certainly is not designed to satisfy a barbaric horror vacui, just as it does not satisfy the need to close up the abyss between human and divine. An interpretation of angelology that followed similar criteria would reduce it to demonology—an essential distinction to which we will return at length later. The Angel, with its manifold connotations (one thinks of Maimonides's synthesis of the meanings of the term),[20] manifests both the inconceivable richness of the Invisible, the infinite names of the No-where and incites the extraordinary vis (power) of imagination dwelling in man. Angel, says Maimonides, is the name of the imaginative faculty once it dialogues *actu* (actively) with the Cherub. The space of angelic Names (Angels or messengers of the Logos, according to Philo, "ideas" of the living God who cannot remain circumscribed within the identity of being with itself)[21] is, indeed, structured according to the image of a ladder or Axis, which traverses the threshold between terrestrial world and spiritual realities. But this image is not to be interpreted in a "physical" sense, as if it were a question of filling, by degrees, some definite container. Here the Invisible ab-solves itself from its concealment.[22] But Truth cannot show itself naked to the world—as Gabriel, the great messenger, the *man* of God, tells Muhammad; Truth is veiled by sev-

enty thousand veils of light and darkness.[23] If Truth suddenly were
to appear to us unveiled (that is, no longer in the form of re-vela-
tion) we would die of it. The Taboric light overwhelms and dis-
heartens even the Apostles, although it is merely the prefiguration
of the final Parousia. Apocalypse is the un-veiling of the Truth;
when it occurs, *ta prota apelthan*, this first world has passed away,
this creation is finished (Revelation 21:4).[24] But for now the myriads of angelic hosts contained in the Jewish mysticism of the
Throne of the Holy One, the hierarchies of Pseudo-Dionysius, the
Islamic Angels all demonstrate a necessity: that Truth must re-veal
itself in Names (in infinite Names) for it to correspond to the
theōrein of humans, so that, in turn, they may comply with it.
Even the "Deo assimilari" (becoming similar to God) of Thomas
Aquinas (*Summa contra Gentiles*, III, 19) does not require the
elimination of the finite character of separate angelic substances.[25]
The object of immediate angelic intuition is neither the material
world in itself, nor the Creator: the Angel contemplates their
nature only *analogically*, that is, in the mirror of its own spiritual
world, of its own aevum (sempiternity). In the Angel, the inner
experience of its own species, the intuition of its own nature, is
absolutely perfect: it is grasped *totum simul* (entirely at once), not
by way of succession and juxtaposition as occurs in humans. But
everything that remains outside the immediate and infused intuition of itself is also contemplated indirectly by the Angel, through
analogy and similitude.[26]

In guiding from visible things to invisible ones, the Angel is
the figure of the *anagogy*, of the sensus anagogicus, that pertains
to future life and heavenly things. This anagogy edifies, better: it
gives grounds to the hope for a heavenly Jerusalem, beyond the
movement of allegory that pertains to the edification of faith,
beyond the movement of tropology that edifies charity. The anagogy can lead hic et nunc (here and now) to a sort of vision of the
eschaton (the last), "ad *contemplanda* mysteria caelestia" (for the
purpose of contemplating celestial mysteries).[27] But no matter how
high it *soars*, it too will never unveil the true Face of God.
"Quaerite faciem eius semper; ut non huic inquisitioni, qua signifi-
catur amor, finem praestet inventio, sed, amore crescente, inquisi-
tio crescat inventi" ("Seek his face evermore; meaning that
discovery should not terminate that seeking, by which love is testi-

fied, but with the increase of love the seeking of the discovered One should increase") (St. Augustine, *Enarratio in Psalmum 104*,3).[28]

The study of Scripture and the ascent through its meanings can conclude in the grace of the ek-stasis represented by the anagogic-angelic flight. The *wings* of the Angel pertain to contemplation.[29] But not even the wings of angelic intelligence, the quickest of all, attain to the identification with the Point of their desire. These wings testify to a spiritual freedom from "service" to the letter and the Law, rather than to the perfect enjoyment of the End. This is also the meaning of the symbol in Dante: the "feathers" free one from the "sirens": "but before the eyes of the full-fledged / in vain is net spread or arrow shot" (*Purgatorio*, XXXI, 43–63).[30] If man can avoid turning "le penne in giuso" ("the wings downwards"), then, like the Angel, he will be able to move "freely" and, by virtue of the strength of his *attentiveness*, be immediately present at the point to which he is spiritually directed; like the Angel, he will finally be able to do whatever *pleases* him: "Take henceforth your pleasure for your guide" (*Purgatorio*, XXVII, 131).[31]

What makes the cosmos into a *uni*-verse is not, therefore, a process of identification, but the analogical-symbolic *religio* that binds its elements, the musical harmony that informs its structure, its being "like numerous chorists associated in one common dance" (Plotinus, *Enneads*, IV, 4, 33). The expression of the "solar eye" has to be understood in this way: the solar eye can attain to the contemplation of the Sun; it is not the Sun. *Although distant*, the eye and the Sun *see each other*. The "physical" distance is eliminated, but not the spiritual difference internalized in the movement of every entity. The attending* to the vision of the Invisible that informs the whole universe prevents any hiatus, but also any identity, between the spiritual and the corporeal. This attending links, level by level and note by note, through the angelic circles and along the Tree of Sefiroth, the terrestrial world to the Face of God—but this Face is only the highest Angel, the Teacher of Abraham, the Angelus faciei (Angel of the Face) of the *Book of Jubilees*,[32] the Metatron of the *Hekhaloth*, of the heavenly Palaces.[33]

The impossibility of attaining the Name through the Names— or, as in Nicholas of Cusa, the possibility of attaining the Name only inattingibiliter (unattainably)—is, for Corbin, the dominant theme of Islamic angelology.[34] In this respect, this angelology reproduces the purest note of Neoplatonic metaphysics, equally distant from any dualistic formulation as from any "assimilative" impatience (present, instead, in the *Corpus Hermeticum*). In the Islamic Angel, Corbin sees the same figure to which Rilke alludes in the famous *Letter to Witwold von Hulewicz* dedicated to the interpretation of the *Duino Elegies*. Does the "intimate and lasting metamorphosis of the visible into the invisible," which appears to Rilke already "perfect" in the Angel,[35] represent the supreme goal of the earthly pilgrimage narrated by Avicenna in his great trilogy?[36] The passage leading from knowledge to theōrein is to be undertaken, according to Avicenna, in imitation of the Angel, as a "production" of the Invisible. This passage bestows on the soul the power to unite with the Light (in accordance with a theme developed in the *Chaldean Oracles* and up to Iamblichus and Proclus), not immediately but through that mirror which the Angel *is*. It reflects to *us* the immutable and indivisible Light, "so subtle that corporeal eyes cannot sustain it" (Iamblichus, *De mysteriis Aegyptiorum*, II, 86), toward which the unquenchable nostalgia of all creatures turns. The Angel educates to this nostalgia for a vision that "no one has ever seen or will ever see" (Pseudo-Dionysius, *De coelesti hierarchia*, IV, 3). Entirely impossible and *only symbolically imaginable* the "Deo assimilari" resonates, for Ibn 'Arabi, in the very name of *Al-Lah*: it is indeed the supreme Name, but, precisely because it is still a name, it is moved incessantly towards the theory of its inaccessible Principle.*[37] The visio facialis (vision of the face) of the Name does not un-veil the Principle.[38] Double and inseparable movement—the entire universe is constituted by the inexhaustible totality of divine Names, which love and love to be loved, which praise and long to find those who praise them. "These orders all gaze upwards and prevail downward, so that toward God all are drawn, and all do draw" (Dante, *Paradiso*, XXVIII, 127–129). The innate desire, which moves all of them toward the Principle of their origin, communicates to each the movement proper to it. Intuiting ineffabiliter (ineffably) the divine nutus (sign), they guide the terrestrial bodies by means of angelic power, (angelica potestate) (St. Augustine, *De libero arbitrio*, III, 11). A musical vision of angelic power will be found again in Thomas Aquinas and Dante. In Augustine, the rhythms (*numbers*) of the angelic souls transmit "legem ipsam Dei . . . usque ad terrena et infra iura" ("the very law of God . . . to the judgments of earth and hell") (*De Musica*, VI, 17; trans. R. Taliaferro, Fathers of the Church, vol. 4, [Washington, D.C.: 1947]); Angels are the names of these rhythms; every Angel is *number* of the Unum Absconditum (Hidden One) that remains, in the Plotinian sense, beyond every determination, and therefore beyond the determination of the One itself. In Dante this musical vision undergoes a decisive re-elaboration: the harmony of the spheres becomes a *polyphonic* discors concordia (discordant harmony). "Paradise is one gigantic concert of instrumental and vocal polyphony in which participate stars, angelic choirs and blessed spirits, and which is divided still more sumptuously into partial choirs, just like a Sacred Symphony of Gabrieli and of Schütz can be at times divided into choirs."[39] One could say that the analogical-symbolic intuition of the universe, the angelological dimension of being (as Corbin calls it), and polyphonic music constitute the names of a single Principle. At the summit of the scale of musical values lies not the numerus sonorus (resounding number) of the Spheres, in the perfect repetitiveness, in the eternal return of its circles, but the sympathy of diverse elements intertwined in the rhythm of a heavenly liturgy. The *Divine Comedy* represents the highest point, in the Western Christian tradition, of such a concept of metaphysically oriented music.[40] This is evident even where a coincidence between angelic notes and the numerus sonorus of the universe is seemingly established. When the Angels intone the Psalm of hope for Dante, who is petrified in front of the "pietade acerba" ("stern pity") of Beatrice, they are indeed designated as "those who ever sing / in harmony with the eternal spheres" (*Purgatorio*, XXX, 92–93), but the notes that they actually follow, their sign, their own trace, appear as "dolci tempre" ("sweet notes") (ibid., 94).[41] Their *sweetly modulated* words are words of hope and mercy, called upon to transform into "spirit and water" "the ice that was bound tight around my heart" (ibid., 97–98). Angelic music accomplishes the *miracle* of this *spiritual transformation* of the numerus sonorus of the Spheres, of the astral necessity "de li etterni giri" ("of the eternal spheres"). One should note here that it is a question of transformation, not of negation—for the "dolci tempre" of angelic liturgy are *in dialogue* with the numerus sonorus of those "etterni giri," and precisely from such dialogue is born the polyphony of the composition.[42]

But what remains of this musical vision in Rilke (that is, in what is perhaps the most vast angelology of the twentieth century)? Precisely the *Duino Elegies* would seem to hinder any simple, linear relation.[43] Although Rilke's term, *Ordnungen* (orders), certainly recalls the Areopagitic hierarchies and, generally, the orthodox angelological tradition[44] (in fact, as we will see, it recalls orthodox iconology more than orthodox theology), the Angels that stand before us in extraordinary relief at the beginning of the *First* and *Second Elegy* do not relate to us with *sympathy*. They do *not* hear my cry, nor could I resist their stronger "Dasein" (existence) if they were suddenly to press me against their heart. The call ("Lockruf") of the Angel is held back, nearly stifled, in a "dark sobbing": "Alas, who is there we can make use of? *Not angels*, not men" (*First Elegy*, 8–10, my emphasis).[45] The choirs of Angels are still beautiful, but we can admire them only because they calmly, "gelassen," do not deign to destroy us. Essentially they have stopped *re-garding* us:[46] if they would do so again, if their attention would strike us again, our Dasein would expire like mist before the light of their beauty.

A light that of necessity is terrible because it reflects the formidable Lumen (Light) of the Principle. "Illuminans tu mirabiliter a montibus aeternis" ("Glorious are thou, more majestic than the everlasting mountains") (Psalm 76:4): with the letters of *na'or* (Lumen) one forms *nora*, which means terrible, terror: "tu terribilis es; et quis resistet tibi?" ("But thou, terrible art thou! Who can stand before thee?") (Psalm 76:7). Perhaps nobody, before Rilke, has heard this word that inextricably joins light and terror with more profound anguish than Turner in his *The Angel Standing in the Sun* of 1846 (clearly inspired by Revelation 19:17). With flaming sword, the Cherub casts away from its vortex of lights the larvae of mortals; its eyes are turned toward some point up there that seemingly escapes it and its mouth is open in a cry or grimace of pain. Even to the Angel its own light sounds terrible.

What role of mediation will the Angel still play? Can its Land-of-no-where still be defined as the place of the encounter, of the reflection unto us of "the divine law itself"? In the *Duino Elegies* the glory of the Angel, the Herrlichkeit of its order, is nothing but the "beginning of Terror": *herrlich* (glorious) and *schrecklich* (terrifying) here form one semantic family.[47] The Angels of Rilke are as beautiful as the ones that appear on the royal Doors, but they turn to the faithful only to prevent their entrance. Their own *tremendous* presence is a sign of distance, of separation. A metaphysical fracture intervenes in the angelological tradition. Instead of being the guardians of a threshold, here Angels appear to be unsurpassable demons of the Limit. The tradition that had always imagined them as guides, interpreters, clarifiers[48] undergoes in the *Duino Elegies* a radical questioning. The image of the Angel is not reduced to a fable nor does its function cease because—as in the rabbinical orthodoxy—one fears the idolatrous aspects of the cult or because—as in the great syntheses of Byzantine theology in Palamas and Cabasilus—it is deemed unnecessary after the Incarnation of the Verbum,[49] but because its figure has been concentrated and absolutized in the terrible figure of the limit which, unsurpassable, afflicts every human Dasein.

From this limit (as if the Angel were always only to say this one word, abstracted from all others: "only the Son has known the Father") rises the invocation to the Angel. Though "knowing what you are"—in other words, though recognizing the separation that has come about, the already consummated Trennung—"I invoke you" (*Second Elegy*, 1–3). The place of the Angel has become this very invocation or, better, the anguish that its unsatisfiability occasions. "Are we not strange creatures to let ourselves go and to be induced to place our earliest affections where they remain hopeless?" (Rilke, *Puppen*).[50] It is with the Angel as it is with the doll-soul, the Puppenseele: when will we ever be able to say that it is *truly present*? Of you, soul of the doll, "one could never say exactly *where* you really were" (ibid., p. 48, English trans.).

The "days of Tobias", when "one of the shining-most" (*Second Elegy*, 3–4), Raphael, inhabitant of the Civitas that has never known any "pilgrimage" (St. Augustine, *De civitate Dei*, XI, 9), closest to the homo in statu viatoris (man in the condition of earthly traveler), as a youth went to the youth to guide and heal them—those days are gone forever.[51] The question posed to Angels, "Who are you?" is still answered by Rilke with tones recovered from the *Celestial Hierarchies* ("dawn-red ridges of all creation"),[52] only to remind us immediately (with as violent a leap as the one that divides, in Hölderlin's *Schicksalslied*, the "soft paths" of "happy genii" from the fading and falling of "afflicted mortals") of the expiration and vanishing "from ember to ember" of our ephemeral beauty. The great play of mirrors that held the angelological dimension of being appears shattered. The light of the "divinity in bloom," which the Angel reflects, closes into itself like a vortex, and it is no longer offered to us in images, detaching itself from the all too weak force of our imaginatio. The "measure" of the Angel ("Those whom you see here were modest," *Paradiso*, XXIX, 58: modesty is the virtue of the limit, and it characterized the faithful Angels that did not fall into the "wretched pride") is pried loose, in Rilke, from the "insistent tension" of our epoch, from its formless ("gestaltlos") character addressed in "das klagende Lied" of the *Seventh Elegy*.[53] "Temples it knows no longer," this epoch; for the temple defines the speculative dimension par excellence, the place that is cut out (temnein-tempus) from the indifferent-equivalent space-time, where the "sea" of Ideas and that of the sensible world converge in mutual, polyphonic resonance.[54] Then how can the destruction of the temple, the production of "spacious garners of power" (*Seventh Elegy*, 55) that lay to "waste" the precincts of the temple, allow us to correspond once again to the figure of the Angel? Where else can the Angel live if not in the mundus imaginalis, in the Imago (image), which the poet says we have lost?

Still, the Angel is invoked. *We* invoke it. The Angel dwells in this invocation, which belongs to our being-here; it dwells on the *earth* where we are. We invoke the Angel so that it may pluck "that small-flowered herb of healing" (*Fifth Elegy*, 58), so that it may find a vase to preserve it "among joys / not *yet* open to us," so that it may tell that we are still *this*: "die Bewahrung (defense, guard, but also testimony, proof) of the still recognizable form (Gestalt)" (*Seventh Elegy*, 66–67). This form is shown "innerlich" (inwardly) by man to the Angel, in the interiority of the invocation he addresses to it. And the Angel ("o du Grosser"), so much larger than us, is astonished by this: it knows nothing of the transformation of the thing into the invisible, of this supreme metamorphosis; it has not led us there, it has not e-ducated us, it can hardly interpret the transformation. *We* show the Angel; we tell to the Angel, and our saying is praise of the *Hiersein*, of the "veins full of existence" of being-here. The invocation is the form of this showing. We do not implore the Angel to lead us and show us; and even if we implored, it could never return to the days of Tobias, come into our sayable, into the time of our sayable things. But, invoking it, we show and tell. Praedica verbum (proclaim the word)[55]—but to the Angel. In saying to the Angel, the word does not flow to the exterior, but interiorizes itself in the image, in the Imago, where the time of succession does not penetrate.[56] "That word is spoken within the mind. 'Pronounce it!': that is, become aware of what is in you" (Meister Eckhart, *Praedica verbum*).[57] There is a word that *one* speaks, the word that comes out of us and becomes rigid in representation, becomes a property of what it designates, which is *deposited* in the designatum (signified). But there is also a word that remains inside whoever pronounces it, like the originary images of creatures remain inside the Father, who is also Logos (Meister Eckhart, *Ave, gratia plena*).[58] The Rilkean Er-innerung* of this mystical "movement" is indubitable: saying to the Angel recollects precisely this pronunciation of the word—we must speak, we must participate in the action of the Verbum and correspond to it, but we return into ourselves through this very saying. To say in such a way so as to invert the sense of the ex-pression and transform it into the recollection of what is inmost in it, "into which time has never penetrated and into which no image has ever cast its reflection" (Meister Eckhart, *Praedica verbum*).[59] That is, to say in such a way that the ex-pression is praise of the invisible, without expecting anything from it, without provoking anything in it. Such saying re-edifies in the heart, invisibly, the thing. The angelic Land of no-where is not if not in us, innerlich. The angelological dimension of being withdraws into the heart of the creature. Meister Eckhart already praises the humility in the nature of the Angel— but here its humility must reach deeper in order to entrust itself to the human word, to the invisible that this word can safeguard. Extreme metamorphosis of the Angel, but *not* its simple disappearance.

The end of the order of the mundus imaginalis does not mean the end of all encounters with the Angel—it means that every encounter will now have to begin by putting ourselves at risk. In the word that implores there resounds the wait for what saves, for a kind of salvation that comes from beyond the misery of the creature. In the invocation, instead, the same voice that invokes also repels: "like an outstretched / arm is my call" (*Seventh Elegy*, 88–89). The invocation *wrestles* with the Angel. Invocation is that of Jacob; invocation is that of Christ at Gethsemane, when he confronts and questions the rigor of the Father without looking for salvation (J. Boehme, *Mysterium Magnum*, LX, 25).[60] To invoke the Angel is to astound it with this strength of the creature in saying its own irredeemable being-there, that is, in *not* imploring. The Angel is astonished by how happy ("glücklich") and "schuldlos" (innocent, but the term has certain echoes that no simple translation can render: not being-cause, to have no aim)[61] such an earthly thing can be, by how things can believe in us, the most fleeting of all creation. We astonish the Angel by showing it the difference between the transformation into the invisible granted to the humility of the word and the Angel's own unsayable. For humans can transform into the invisible *only by saying*. They save the thing only in that Er-innerung which their word can be, can risk itself to become. The word is what transforms into the invisible by interiorizing the thing, hence: praedica verbum. "In the midst of Fate, the extinguisher" (*Seventh Elegy*, 68), the thing can resurrect in the life of the word. But for this to happen, the usual movement must be inverted: the word cannot flow away toward the thing, transform itself into it, "substitute" for it—but the thing has to penetrate into the invisible that is the spiritus of the word. We are here for the sake of saying—but to say in this form, measured against the terrible distance of the Angel, a saying that is Er-innerung. House and Bridge, Door and Window, Column and Tower and Fountain and Tree—all our artifacts together with what we have found, *are*, but are in that place ("Ort," *not* Raum!) which "I can carry in the heart" (*Fifth Elegy*, 73) and therefore which I can only remember by heart.*

To invoke is to struggle with the unsayable. To the Angel's unsayable, this terrible beauty, we show the thing saved in the invisible. Risking ourselves in the terrible ("schrecklich"), terrifying ("furchtbar"), and dangerous ("gefährlich") struggle with the unsayable, we can find the humble word that is the Er-innerung of the thing. That is why the earth and things entrust themselves to us, the most fleeting, and not to the Angel—but only insofar as we risk ourselves in the struggle with the Angel. The word that is Er-innerung can be pronounced only *in* this struggle. In this way there endures in Rilke a necessity of the Angel. If in Rilke no trace is left of the Angel's triumphal image,[62] neither can the figure of the fugitive, the expiration from "ember to ember," be said apart from this invocation-repulsion of the Angel. The initiator-hermeneut Angel, the *Shaykh* Angel of Avicenna and Suhrawardi does not guide the fugitive because the figure of the fugitive is metaphysically distinguished from the one of the pilgrim; it is the *other* of Tobias. But what the fugitive has to say is still always an attempt at the unsayable, a testing of all that is sayable. Therefore the danger of the Angel never leaves the fugitive. The Angel in itself no longer manifests itself, but its image must irrupt into the order of our trying-to-say as an ineluctable *problem*. Paradoxical, antinomical angelology, where fragments or sparks of the accomplished human-divine hierarchies, of their "modest" harmonies by now flash like signs of mourning, as if, like the rest of things, they asked us just to be remembered (ri-cor-dati). As if the Angel, now, implores us who invoke it.

The Angel's kenosis (emptying out) had already begun in *Das Buch der Bilder*.[63] Its name "is like an abyss, a thousand nights deep," to whom I can only stretch out my arms, for "how can I call you?" (*Der Schutzengel*). Terrible and so very high—but already "fallen" in as much as this name is unpronounceable. The Angel is the beginning "which pours itself greatly / I am the slow and fearful Amen"—but how can this Amen, this miserable "frame," compare with the Angels, these "intervals" in the melody of the Lord's garden (*Die Engel*)? The same theme of distance and nostalgia also appears in the splendid *Verkündigung*, in the words that the Angel addresses to Mary; but the difference that separates the two figures is now comprehended in another, infinitely more vast: the difference that averts both from God, "wir sind ihm all weit" ("we are all far from him"). The Angel is weary; the way was so long, the vertigo of the fall so violent that it has forgotten what it had to announce, what it had heard up there, by the Throne of gold and jewels. Now it stands immense in the little house, unable to praedicare verbum. Mary is lonelier than ever, she hardly notices the presence of the one who should have greeted her with these words: "the Lord is with you." The Angel is the beginning, the origin, the day; it has seen and heard—but now it depends on the "slow and fearful Amen." The Angel is ungraspable and unsayable like the first instant of the day or the first drop of dew ("ich bin der Tau")—but now its destiny lies with the "plant." That beginning, that instant now have to pass through its "door." The Angel with immense wings and great robes is but a wind. She *meditates* ("du Sinnende") on the unsayable annunciation that this wind carries; her soul tries to listen and welcome it. In this way she is transformed into the plant of the spiritus that flashed for one instant, barely remembering itself, confused by the space it had traversed, in her miserable home or in her dream.

The figure of the Angel lasts only the time of this listening, in the meditation and invocation that the listening concentrates in itself. And would not our struggle with the Angel, which is shown, precisely, in the form of the invoking meditation, then be its "salvation"? The Angel that comes in the night "to test you by struggling with you" (*Der Engel*, in *Neue Gedichte* [English translation, Rainer Maria Rilke, *New Poems*, trans. J. B. Leishman (New York: Hogarth Press, 1964)]) undoubtedly wants to seize you and "wrench you from your retaining mould," as if it had created you; but the Angel itself arrives *thirsty* from the extreme distance of its no-where. Its gaze seems *dry*,[64] and only from our features can it drink "the clear wine of faces." "Steinerner" (*L'Ange du Méridien, Chartres*), of stone, is the Angel: what does it know "of our being"? But *our* flood can inundate its gaze. It has come out of the powerful wheel of what eternally returns, expelled from the rose windows of the ancient cathedral, from the original expanse of the Realm where "a casual point can have no place" (*Paradiso*, XXXII, 53). Only its thirst is left of the word it had to announce. *This* the Angel addresses *to us*; with it we have to wrestle. To entrust ourselves into the hands of the Angel would mean to be ravished into the pure unsayable. But to measure ourselves with its thirst is our "number," the "modesty" that is proper to our saying. It is as if the Angel imparted its unsayable to our word and to its power of transfiguring innerlich the thing—as if even for the Angel, ancient master of measure, the only salvation lay in the "circumspection of the human gesture," the Aidōs (reverence) forever remembered in the Attic stela (*Second Elegy*, 66).[65]

2

ANGEL
AND
DEMON

These angels no longer draw solely "from what is theirs": "a little of our existence" is mixed with them "as though through an oversight" (*Second Elegy*, 31–33). They are not aware of it, but it so happens that something uncertain is added to their traits, something that has our flavor.[1] The wave we produce in dissolving just reaches their "cosmic space" (*Second Elegy*, 30). The orientation of the Angel vacillates; it has lost forever the rigidity of the Gnostic Archon, of the celestial Souls in Avicenna, lost the omniscience of the Angels of Hekhaloth, constellated with eyes each as vast as the moon's sphere. Formerly the Angel spoke: "eveniet ut . . ." ("it will come to pass that . . ."), and the clarity of the message overcame all anxiety, polarizing our attention and demanding action, drān*: "Non possum . . . sed fiat." ("I cannot . . . but let it happen.") Now the Angel descends into our exile; the struggle with it retains it in our passage, in our Passagenwerk—just as the struggle uproots us from every possible dwelling, lasting, trusting in a mother earth, so it prevents the Angel from returning, from spreading its great wings. Riveted to our invocation-rejection, it is suspended and confused. The Angel that was to *induce* us to the Land-of-no-where, that was sent to us for this purpose from the nonplace of the Origin, has been slowly *seduced* by our continuous fleeing far from everything "wie ein luftiger Austausch," like an aerial exchange, a changing wind (*Second Elegy*, 74–79), the only spiritus of our "little strip of orchard" that can no longer appease itself in "godlike bodies," which we may only seek after. To draw from human exis-

15

tence means, for the Angel, to reflect our questions and share our extreme distance from that no-where of the full answer, to which the Angel yet belongs. Our "flavor" makes the Angel forgetful. Drinking the "clear wine" of our traits, it forgets the rope that held it fixed to the Principle. The measure of its circles, the order and taxis of its whirlwind become a labyrinth. The play of mirrors between the divine and the terrestrial, which the Angel's logos seemed to represent in harmonious correspondences, refracts into sudden dissonances. Voids, accidents, and the unforseen irrupt into it. Down here the music of the Angel, that of the struggle in which we invoke it, is composed of such dissonances. Still an Angel, the nostalgia for the Point that transcends every name persists in its root; although it still invites us on the journey to this no-where, it can no longer tell us about its stages or anticipate any of its moments. Its science (symbolized by the myriads of eyes in its celestial body[2]) has been clouded by reflecting on the mirror of our ignorance or due to our being always turned backward, forced to look behind our backs, withdrawn in the gesture of a perennial farewell (*Eighth Elegy*, 70–75). The Angel, too, has forgotten to look into the Open, "ins Freie." Although it was this look that answered our question and, in the same instant, allowed for the Angel's return into itself, to the perfect order of the Caelum Caeli. Forgetful, the Angel can only remain down here. The human invocation-rejection represents for the Angel an unsurpassable *scandal*. One and the same adventure engulfs the two figures—and at the end, in spite of itself, the Angel falls in love with the struggle to which it was invoked.

But the possibility of this catastrophe—that the Angel be seduced instead of being the one who induces—runs like a continuous bass, dark and menacing, along the whole itinerary of angelology. From its first appearance, man represents a crossroad for the Angel: the originary order of the heavenly court is from the start overwhelmed by it. The first Angel to be created (even before Micheal, ut Deus), head of the twelve Angels defenders of the Throne, cannot submit—being made of fire—to the adoration of the clot of clay and matter kneaded by the Lord.[3] This decision, this "cursed pride" lacerates forever the preceding harmony. It is the irreversible division of the angelic choir that appears tragic and not so much the destiny of that particular prince and of its following.

In *Bereshit Rabbah*, VIII, 5 (English trans., J. Neusner, *Genesis Rabbah* [Atlanta: Scholars Press, 1985], p.79), the Angels are still discussing the matter, uncertain between the mercy that invites to the creation of man and the truth that dissuades from doing so, when the Lord *decides* (archetype of the Sovereign who decides on the state of emergency!): "What good are you doing [with your contentions]? Man has already been made!" This demonstrates that *no* Angel could have been really convinced of the goodness of such a creation. Some are obedient to the brute fact of the divine decision, others rebel against it. The rebellion takes the form of a *revenge* for the tear in the heavenly network (and, at bottom, in the relationship between the Angel and its ineffable Principle) provoked by the creation of man. Just as this network was "seduced" from its perfect circular orbit around the Throne, so now the fallen Angel will try with every means to seduce humankind from all works of goodness and peace: "I will seduce all men except Your faithful servants" (*Koran*, XXXVIII, 82–83 [English trans., N. J. Dawood (New York: Penguin Books, 1956)]), "I will waylay Your servants as they walk on Your straight path, and spring upon them from the front and from the rear, from their right and from their left" (ibid., VII, 16–17). The seductions performed by the Islamic Iblis,[4] the talmudic Samael, Angel of death and chief of the Satanim, are the reflection and supplicium (torture) of the *scandal* that man represented for the entire Heavenly court.

Even the image of the most faithful Angel bears evident traces of its painful doubt with respect to the novitas (novelty) of man[5] (authentic *decision* of creation!); even the messenger Angel is not exempt from the doubt. In the presence of its Majesty, having finally left at sunset the earth entrusted to its care, the Angel *cries*: "We have come from those who have called on thy name, whom the difficulties of the world have made miserable; for every hour they devise many opportunities, not making one pure prayer, not even with the whole heart, all the time they live; *why therefore must we be present with men who are sinners?*" ("The Apocalypse of Paul," my emphasis).[6] The very presence of man torments the Angel, both the messenger and guardian Angel (including the Archangel that with profound sympathy recounts to the King the unspeakable suffering of humans, the violence that they undergo and perform "because of You, the Only One they worship in every thing that they adore," in the "Prologue" to *De pace fidei* of Nicholas of Cusa,) as well as the fallen Angel, condemned to survive until Judgment Day—for this much time God has allotted it in order to seduce, accuse, inflict the penalty of death, and avenge itself of its own catastrophe.

The other major crisis suffered by the Angel because of man, vaguely alluded to in Genesis 6:1–4,[7] is narrated in the *Book of Guardians*, first part of the *Book of Enoch*, which exerted an enormous influence on the early Church. To join with the daughters of men, some of the Angels, creatures of the first day, renounce their condition and *freely* choose to abandon Heaven. The Angel falls in love with woman, goes to her and with her begets Giants that torment the earth and devour its creatures (*Book of Enoch*, VI–XI). Enoch, whose figure will be metamorphosed into that of an angel in the Hekhaloth (the very mysticism of Metatron centers on his metamorphosed figure),[8] is sent by God to reprimand their impiety and announce their punishment. They were "spiritual, living the eternal life and immortal for all generations of the world," they had "their dwelling in Heaven" (*Book of Enoch*, XV:7–8) but the beauty of the daughters of men made them fall; for this sin they will be kept eternally in a horrible place, a prison full of great descending columns of fire, and the women with them (ibid., XXI:7–8). The narrative in the *Book of Jubilees*, although based on the *Book of Enoch*, emphasizes the role played by the human creature in the seduction of the Angel.[9] While in the *Book of Guardians* the beauty of woman is merely noticed and the Angel's intention moves by itself toward evil, in the *Book of Jubilees*, instead, God sends the Angel to earth, which already knew sin, and *on earth* the Angel shatters its own law. Here it is human beings that teach the Angel how to sin. The revenge that the fallen Angel or its demons will try to wreak on them will have to be all the more horrible.[10]

In *De Gigantibus* (English trans., D. Winston, *The Giants* [New York: Paulist Press, 1981]), Philo tries to "absolve" the Angel from the drama of this fall. It is superstition, he says, to believe in Angels that are "impious and unworthy of their name." The Angel is only the ambassador of God to humans and of humans to God; it is sacred and inviolable. Only the souls of men marry women and beget Giants, they "have had no regard for wisdom. . . . They have surrendered themselves to unstable and chance concerns . . . to that corpse which was our birth-fellow." These souls fly in the air together with Angels as well as with those other souls that, even though they descend into the sensible world, nonetheless "practice dying to the life in the body" (these are the souls of philosophers). The air is full of such invisible beings. Drawing life from the air and the wind, all terrestrial and aquatic animals communicate with demons, Angels, and souls.[11] But the allegorical interpretation of Philo reduces all too transparently the figure of the Giant to that of man, who has deserted the alliance with God, "without family or fatherland, vagabond and exile," in order to cast authentic light on the drama of the Angel. In particular, this interpretation poses a problem that it does not solve: in this world "animated from one end to the other," what is the relation between the Angel and the demon? Are they entities distinguished only by name? Or are they different entities that share a common essence? If the Angel, as one can deduce from the cited passage, is only the sacred and inviolable ambassador, what is the origin of evil demons? Are they one with those human souls that cannot re-emerge from the violent vortex of fortuitous and unstable things? Or are they, instead, the name given by philosophers to the fallen Angels? The Platonic allegory of Philo, precisely in its explicit attempt to "demystify" the biblical tradition, "probes" in a mythical sense the image of the Angel, imposing the problem of its relation with the pagan demon.

But before following this new meander, it is necessary to insist on what every tradition brings to light: a gravitational force endangers the angelic Sphere. A force that is essentially different from the irresistible, narcissistic impulse that takes hold of the hermetic Anthropos, son of the Father, and condemns him to fall into a union with Nature (*Poimandres, Corpus Hermeticum I*, 12–14). The Anthropos pursues his own image, reflected on the Earth's water, even after it has managed to surpass the circle of the Moon; the Angel, instead, is touched by the wave of the human invocation; it is seized and forced beyond its own measure by *another* voice, another image. Nor is the Angel's journey of intercession ever assured. Each one of its journeys in some way always "imitates" those archetypal falls. Nor is the human invocation ever "pure": the invocation is always impregnated with our "flavor," which is seductive to the Angel. From this arise the differences and dissonances, misunderstandings and equivocity, the irresolvable play of affinity and distance, the possibility of confusing roles, of exchanging masks. The meeting places with the Angel belong neither to the perfect blindness of Samael (God of the blind) nor to the triumphal entrance into the reign of Light. In these places, man wavers between the Angel and the bestial figure of the Giants; and the Angel, in turn, wavers between the *visio facialis* and the aerial demon, between the closest proximity to the Presence (Metatron at times is identified with the Shekhinah) and the idolatrous images of archons, as told in the extraordinary imaginatio of the *Pistis Sophia* and other Gnostic texts.[12] An infinite number of intermediate beings can be called upon to bridge these distances: an immense space, so densely populated (we saw this in Philo) that its complete exegesis becomes problematical, and the figure of the Angelus Interpres itself becomes an unreachable telos of creation. Even Proclus "has to be read by overturning the canonic principle consecrated by medieval scholasticism":[13] for him, entia sunt multiplicanda ex necessitate (beings are to be multiplied out of necessity). The intermediate levels, the processions of beings, guarantee the theophantic unity of the cosmos, unite the world of becoming to the Principle, and make the part share in the Whole. Without a *science* of the "unified plurality" (*Elementa theologiae*, 128) of the Henads, the cosmic harmony would be torn into infernal dissonances (justifying in this case the dualistic gnosis that refuses to recognize not only animated and thinking bodies but also divine ones; see ibid., 129). And yet the same principle of multiplication of beings ex necessitate leads to the necessary construction-imagination of a space whose relations and "sympathies" are so labyrinthine that its very hierarchy is rendered ineffable and unknowable. (Does this not also explain the theurgic dimension of Neoplatonic thought?) One has to comprehend the last, great encounters with the Angel against the background of this drama. There is a fever, an originary antinomy in angelology that imperiously returns in these encounters and that no law can govern anymore.

One of these last "stations" of the Angel is drawn by Klee. He multiplies its names, renders its entanglement with demons and souls, comprehends its drama with a desperate irony. Here our "flavor" has forever re-vealed the Angel, who tries in vain to extricate itself from it. This "station" succeeds the one of Rilke, although they share a profound affinity. The Er-innerung has dissipated the tremendous distance that resonated at the beginning of the *Duino Elegies*, and now it refracts in imperceptible differences, in minimal variations around the theme of the Angel's complete *creatureliness*: the names Klee gives to it are those of the Angel-mere-creature. Our struggle with it, our Er-innerung, have transformed it into what is most intimate to the creature: the "pampered darlings of Creation" (*Second Elegy*, 10) now know what their privilege concealed—to have to attain the heart of the creature; to have to interiorize themselves in it. The signs of the plant—roots, branches, lymph—by now envelop the Angel from every side. It still seems capable of safeguarding (see the drawings from 1931 on the theme of *Engelshut*), but by now its ample wings, its step, the eyes all form a single labyrinth with the figures comprehended in it. It has become impossible to distinguish to whom belongs that walk, if that is indeed the Angel's wing. The steps of Raphael and Tobias by turns invoke and reject each other—as if both, reciprocally and together, guided and seduced one another.

The theme of the Engelshut (Angel's guard) has a certain affinity with that of the *Angelus Militans* (1940), an Angel that never rests, emblem of the undistracted *prosochē* (attention) characteristic of orthodox mysticism: Angel of the wake, of the restless Agrypnia (insomnia). Against a black background stand out the white outlines of *Wachsamer Engel* (1939), the great open eyes shine, and it stirs its ready wings.[14] The estote parati ("you shall be prepared!") of the "angelic life" of oriental monasticism[15] seems also to transpire through the symmetrical balance of the Angel illuminated by the Star, of 1939, or of the Angel oriented around the sign of the Cross and that *becomes* in accord with this sign (*Engel im Werden*, of 1934). The prosochē of these figures demonstrates their faith: for the Angels must also *believe*. They cannot identify with the Glory, nor contemplate it directly. (Only the Son has known the Father—but not even the Son knows "de die autem illo vel hora" [the day or the hour]: the Angel does not surpass human knowledge with respect to the eschaton).[16] Like the man of faith, so the Angel: it listens to a voice without words, contemplates an Invisible, waits for a day of which it knows nothing.[17]

This Christian-oriental angelology recovers motifs already present in postbiblical Jewish literature: one thinks of the indefatigable guardians, the last rose of light of the world of Sefiroth, the threshold between that world and the terrestrial one. But precisely their extreme distance from the highest Angel (which is the Face sent by God to the chosen people in *Exodus*; the Face that, according to Kabbalistic interpretations, is manifest in the Three that appear to Abraham) makes these last Angels dangerously similar to man: spirits that preside over the elements rather than Cherubic intelligences, "ea luce illuminati, qua creati" ("being illumined by the Light that created them") (St. Augustine, *De civitate Dei*, XI, 9). Their traits border on those of the demon—or on those of the human soul forced into interminable pilgrimages and reincarnations. The terms distinguishing these dimensions of being become indistinct. The adventure of the Angel in Klee is reminiscent of the Archangel's "descent," indicated by Iamblichus in the following terms: from the gods to the Archangel, from the Archangel to the Angel, from this to the demon, to the hero, to the archon (in charge of the direction of matter), and so on down to the souls most distant from the superior regions, down to the vain apparitions of ghosts, the fatuous fires of deceiving magic, the "fallacious alterations" of the "various genera" (Iamblichus, *De mysteriis Aegyptiorum*, II, 84–95). These spaces are extraordinarily animated, they pullulate with entities that are imperceptible to our senses. "The whole air is full of souls which are called demons or heroes; these are they who send men dreams and signs of future disease and health, and not to men alone, but to sheep also and cattle as well" (Diogenes Laertius, *Lives*, VIII, 32; English trans., R. D. Hicks, [Cambridge, Mass.: Harvard University Press, 1972])—but what order informs this life? What Nomos (law) does it manifest? How is its mediating function, its *metaxy*, internally articulated?

Confronted with these questions, the Angels of Klee confess their own ignorance. No matter how solid and sober their figure sometimes appears, no matter how attentive their gaze seems, they spy, but do not reflect, the Light whose emanation they confusedly remember themselves to be. Maybe they are still immortal, but certainly not the "dawn-red ridges of all creation." As guardians and custodians they remain riveted to the threshold. They know the heart of the "sanctuary" as little as we do. If they have ever gone beyond that limit and visited inside, they have forgotten it—and have forgotten that they forgot. The strongest among them accompany man up to the threshold; they watch him waiting. They envy his hope—envy the necessity of his questioning and invoking. And here again, the presence of man overwhelms them. Reflecting his misery, Angels can be overwhelmed by an irresistible self-pity; forced as they are to "serve" the desperate waiting of man; forced to "make up" answers that in reality transform the question into an interminable chain of images and problems. Until, weary, they are forced to confess—precisely to man, the most fleeting being in creation—their own impotence.[18]

This *fallen* guardian Angel absorbs, in Klee, the other images of traditional angelology. Here no traces are left of the Areopagitic hierarchies or of the initiatory-eschatological visions found in Iranian-Islamic mysticism. Klee concentrates his attention on the dimensions of angelology that are most "implicated" with the transience and fallenness of the mundus sitalis. The Angel of Klee is caught in a vortex that forces it to flee the angelic macromirror. A centrifugal force that moves it from inside wrenches it from the "fiery love" of the Seraphim (*Paradiso*, XXVIII, 45), from the scorching intelligence of Suhrawardi's hermeneut Angel, from the intense blue sky of the Cherubic choir[19] (symbol, in Pseudo-Dionysius, of the disposition to knowledge and contemplation) toward our "chemins qui ne mènent nulle part" ("roads leading nowhere") (quoting from Rilke and not Heidegger!).[20] The great catastrophes of the angelic court in the end have managed to cast every Angel *into crisis* (pencil drawings of 1939), *into doubt* (*Angelus dubiosus*, watercolor of 1939). In these sheets, the Angel withdraws like a frightened nocturnal bird; too inexperienced to guard or guide, it tries in vain to find refuge within the bosom of its own wings. We surprise it resting in the *Antechamber of the host of Angels* (title of a 1939 drawing): debutante-Angel, or ex Angel, it aspires to return to the Land-of-no-where, with the face illuminated melancholically by a pale crescent of the moon (*Engel-Anwarter*): Angel-Pierrot. It is a poor Angel in spite of the *mania* (madness) that still at times, suddenly, makes it praedicare verbum: fragments, traces, sparks of the Message that it ought to have signified. Hence its own form is incomplete (*Unfertiger Engel*): it participates in toto (fully) in the incompleteness of the whole creation.

Incompleteness means metamorphosis, change of roles, ironic dissolution of the certainty of figures, of their "ubi" (where). Not only can the Message turn out, at the end, to be unproclaimable—but the Messenger can also forget *itself* on reaching the end of its journey (not because it knows this to be the true end to which it is destined, but because it is by now too tired, too lost to continue). The Messenger can still name itself ("Ein Bote bin ich" is the answer Barnabas gives to K. in *The Castle*); but how can its figure and its words disentangle themselves from the incomplete (interminable?) game of creation? We are left with the impatience of our waiting, the necessity of our questioning. "From early morning to sunset I have walked up and down my room"; "by dint of looking I knew its every trifle."[21] And now, finally, the room begins to move; large breaches open its walls; waves of color invade its space, colors of the manifestation: radiant white, yellow, yellow-gold. "This was intended for me, there was no doubt; an appearance (Erscheinung) was being prepared that would *free me*" (my emphasis). That which wanted to come was descending toward me to anounce what it had to announce. "An Angel then! I thought. All day it flies towards me and I, sceptic as I am, did not know it. Now it will speak to me." But instead of the word, the verbum, the Annunciation there occurs the transformation, the metamorphosis, the *change of scene*—or, better, the very announcement of this change of scene. An instant after the apparition of the Angel "dressed in violet-blue clothing, girded with golden cords, with large white wings of silken splendour, the sword brandished horizontally in its lifted hand," an eye-wink after that instant, it is no longer a "living Angel" that is poised under the roof of the room, but a painted wooden figure, like those suspended in taverns of sailors. The hilt of the sword served as a candlestick and "under the weak light of the Angel, I remained seated until night."

Kafka does not describe a hallucination or a mirage. The Angel *appears* in its descent from high above into the room already "measured" in all of its dimensions; the figurehead of painted wood *appears*. Lastly, the candlelight still may be called the "weak light of the *Angel*." Just as in Klee's figures, every angelic "substance" dissolves—but the ironic dissolution does not coincide at all with the negation of the Angel. On the contrary, the Angel is precisely the message of this dissolution; it announces the dissolution of its own "substance" in the metamorphosis of its signs. But in this dissolution, uncertain, never safe, wavering between presence and oblivion, melancholic because of the studium sine fine (endless study) that its own figure evokes, the Angel does not desist from signaling the problem of the representation of its own ou-topia, which is, as we will see, the problem of representation tout court. In this page of Kafka's diary we find the most traditional and stereotyped triumphant Angel together with the most traditional and stereotyped of profane images, entangled in the knot of the most desperate paradox (which the presence of irony, far from annihilating it, surrenders to an unbridgeable distance). These are the extreme poles, the limit-masks, so to speak, that embrace the Angels-in-transformation and the Augenblicksgötter (gods of the instant) ceaselessly imagined by Klee.

But one figure, above all, seems to collect, in Klee, the different names of the Angel: that of the Angelus Novus. This figure makes the reference to talmudic angelology, with the richness of its visionary and fabulous elements, not just pertinent but obligatory. Only Michael and Gabriel (axis of the Tree of the Sefiroth) perennially serve God and glorify the ineffable Light; all the other Angels sing their hymn and then disappear, returning where they were created, in the river of fire (Daniel 7:10), which like the Jordan never ceases to flow, day or night, as it is produced by the sweat of the four Hayoth of Ezekiel's vision while they support the Throne of the Holy One. Also Maimonides will return to this tradition in the angelological sections of his *Guide of the Perplexed* to give it a philosophical explanation: just as each entity possesses an individual formative force that shapes and structures its limbs, so two Angels cannot perform the same mission, nor one Angel carry out two of them. Each event has its Angel, "every force appertaining to the bodily forces is an angel" (*Guide*, II, 6; Pines trans., p. 264). But then why distinguish the permanent and stable Angels from the fleeting ones? When speaking of stable Angels one means the *species* of individual forces; when speaking of fleeting Angels, the individual forces as such. The New Angel is, so to speak, the image of the Angel immanent to the most singular and unrepeatable individuality of the creature—better, the New Angel is the name of the *force* that makes this single being-there unrepeatable and unique.

Once this "station" is reached, the symbolism of the Angel cannot be disentangled from that of the creature. The symbolism of the passage, essential to every angelology, here coincides with the very icon of the Angel. The Angel no longer "passes," transmits, and intercedes, but is itself the passage: icon of the *in-stant* itself (again that thin strip of earth, between rock and river, which *insists* between rock and river, of which speaks the *Second Elegy?*). In the likeness of the Lord's Day, the New Angel, suspended in its being-instant, does not linger behind but exercises *patience* in it,[22] attentive to the unrepeatable moment of its hymn. The Nunc aeternum (eternal now) of the Angel's aevum, which it knew "in a light that is above all time" (Meister Eckhart), the same Nunc in which it could contemplate *totum simul* on its mirror without blemishes, has turned into the elusive flash of the instant. But precisely this— the elusive—is what the New Angel signals. Elusive is that single force which moves this single, unique entity; elusive is the minimal wind that yet constitutes each voice; elusive, too, are the spirits that yet animate each space and join themselves to each element. The New Angel is the elusive *reality* of which lives the individual being-there.[23] This is why the individual force is said to be an Angel, that is, invisible and elusive. The fallenness of this New Angel (which, in Klee's drawing, faces us and carries on its brow the scrolls of the Law) renews ours by *re-creating* it. The figure of this Angel expresses the strength to think and praise the instant, the strength to paint *icons* of the passage itself and poverty itself. Authentic icons of the time of misery are thus given. Things must be said to the Angel—but said to the New Angel—because, of all its names, only this one expresses what is most fleeting and fallen (characteristic of our things, of our being-here) as the realissimum (the most real). In meditating-interiorizing (er-innern) his own fallenness, man encounters the New Angel, which is the figure of it. The Angel figures the force of the fallen instant, the force that makes the instant *stand* in its unrepeatable singularity, that frees it from the continuum of the succession of moments. The New Angel is thus much more than the merely inexperienced or incomplete Angel: it *stands* in the nunc of its moment. Maybe in its space it has truly absorbed the "warm, fugitive wave of the heart" that we are, so as to express finally its irrevocable present:

But this
having been *once*, though only *once*:
having been once on *earth*—can it ever be cancelled?
(*Ninth Elegy*, 14–16).[24]

Its hymn, lasting only for an instant, is not dis-cursive, it does not place sound after sound and word after word on the arrow-line of irreversible consumption. The New Angel is an *infant*: it does not demand, or ask, or question. It is *schuldlos* (innocent). At times it seems "content" with its impotence in being a means, a cause, an end. It is "simple" like the sound of hand-bells (*Schellen-Engel*, drawing of 1939). It is the youngest of the musician Angels:[25] the harmony of the spheres is not its burden; and yet its song is no less clear, its *mania* no less intense. The New Angel lives in the kinder-garten (*Engel im Kindergarten*, of 1939): here our invocation reaches it; here it recognizes what we praise in it; here we wrestle with it. As if the fragility of infancy finally transfigures itself into the strength to resist all dis-coursing. This infancy of the Angel produces *lucida intervalla* (clear intervals): holes, ruptures, tears in the apparent continuum of Time-Kronos. In this sense, the "birth of the Savior," archetype of infancy, already represented the victory over *Heimarmenē* (fate), over the stars and astrology (Clement of Alexandria, *Excerpta ex Theodoto*, 74–78).

The New Angel is the last figure (risked with the most diffi-cult-desperate irony) of the great angelological theme, of Neopla-tonic ancestry, opposing the angelic Nous to Moira (fate), mistress of demons.[26] This contrast marks the whole adventure of the Angel: its vicissitudes coincide with the repetition, in different forms, of the attempt to disentangle itself from the affinity with the demon, and remove the terrible danger posed by the appearance of a com-mon origin. And yet was not the figure of the *daimon* developing, in the Greco-Roman world, toward the function of metaxy, of medi-ation and intercession?[27] In Plutarch (in *De Genio Socratis* and elsewhere) the daimon can come to the aid of man.[28] Its discourse without voice (*De Genio Socratis*, 588e; English trans. P. De Lacy, *On the Sign of Socrates*, in *Plutarch's Moralia*, vol. 7; [Cambridge, Mass:: Harvard University Press, 1959]) is only perceptible by minds that are pure and free from passions: "we define these men sacred and demonic" (593f). The demon's desire to save the souls of those who have "in the course of countless births bravely and resolutely sustained a long series of struggles" (593f) certainly belongs neither to the Homeric daimon nor to that of Hesiod. This is a development of soteriological themes pertaining to Pythagorean and Platonic demonology.[29] Even the simple mediating function of the daimon cannot be attested to prior to these developments.[30] In Homer the term *daimon* seems to be distinguished from that of *theos*, "in that it defines an indistinct divine agent rather than a divinity individuated in cult and myth";[31] under theos is thought the god's personality as defined by cult and mythology, under daimon, instead, is thought its effect, its power: the numen (will) of the god. In Hesiod the daimon is clearly distinguished from the gods, lords of Olympus, and defines a species of beings unknown to Homer: the souls of the first race of men who lived happily under Kronos, "of strong arms and legs, free from all evils, they passed their lives in feasts, and died as if tricked by sleep," and now "are on earth" as guardians of the works of mortals (Hesiod, *The Works and Days*, 113; trans. Richmond Lattimore [Ann Arbor: University of Michigan Press, 1959]). But not even in Hesiod do the daimons assume a role of mediation or intercession: the souls of those who died in the Golden Age guard and preserve the works of humans as ministers of cosmic Dike (justice). They act wisely (one ought to recall the Platonic etymology in the *Cratylus* that makes explicit reference to this passage in Hesiod) respectful of the *metra* (proportions) of Dike.

The daimon, for Plato, is "something between god and mortal" (*Symposium*, 202e; trans. Michael Joyce [Princeton, N.J.: Princeton University Press, 1985])—and precisely Diotima's discourse sketches out for it a possible mediating function. It has the power to "interpret and convey messages to the gods from men and to men from the gods, prayers and sacrifices from the one, and commands and rewards from the other" (202e). The background remains the mythical one of a space full of demons, the animated Whole; but detached from it there is a definite category of beings characterized by a particular and irreplaceable mediating function (this will also be the case in Plotinus, *Enneads*, III, 5). The god never communicates directly with man but only through the demonic (from which derive divinations and sacrifices, as well as spells and prophecies). For men in this age, once the progeny of the

Golden Age has disappeared underground, the relation to the god is entrusted to the power of the daimon.

How does this concept of daimon fit in with Platonic psychology and eschatology? The soul is clearly distinguished from the daimon. On such a distinction is based the possibility—formulated in the famous passage of the *Republic*—for the soul to *choose* its own daimon. This possibility, in turn, grounds every soteriological-eschatological perspective. The "origin" of that thoroughly problematic path, adumbrated in Plato and fully developed in Plotinus and Proclus, that frees the soul from the kyklos tēs geneseōs, from the fatal wheel of generation, from the constraint of the eternal return,[32]—the "origin" of every idea of salvation is precisely that decision which the soul can make in front of Lachesis, before it plunges again into a new, ephemeral corporal existence, "prelude to a new death" (*Republic*, X, 617e; trans. Paul Shorey [Princeton, N.J.: Princeton University Press, 1985]). In this extremely *critical* instant, the soul can avoid *repeating* its past existence and can choose its own life on the basis of what it has seen and learned. The cycle of reincarnations is marked by this critical instant; if the soul confronts it with ever-increasing *science*, the cycle can be transformed into a process of purification. This possibility, in any case, constitutes the presupposition of every idea of final redemption.

The soul is "free" with respect to the daimon: the responsibility of the choice lies solely with it, not with the god, not with the Moirai (fates), and not with chance that establishes the order in which souls have to choose. "Aitios o elomenos," in my choice lies the cause. "Virtue has no master" (ibid.). But once the choice is made, Lachesis gives as a companion to each soul the demon that it has chosen, and this union is made binding by Clotho and Atropos (ibid., 620e). For the duration of its future incarnation nothing will change the soul. What decides of life is not decided in life, but in the fatal moment that precedes rebirth. The course of life is wholly necessitated by what happens in this moment of extreme peril ("There seems to lie, dear Glaucon, the whole danger for man"). Binding indissolubly the soul to the demon, the Moirai only affirm the irreversible character of the soul's choice: they "execute" the destiny that it chose, fixing the soul to this destiny through an inexorable guardian. In the course of its new existence, the daimon will reveal itself to the soul in interiore homine (in man's interiority) (and a demonic person, like Socrates, will clearly discern its peremptory voice), but only to confirm the soul within the limits, within the furrow that it freely chose for itself, before falling into the body again, before being born *to a new death*—precisely to prevent the soul from wandering off the inalterable path (for this turn of the wheel of Necessity) to which Atropos has bound it.

Also in Plutarch the demon maintains its objectivity with respect to the soul. The souls that Timarchus sees falling down like stars to a new birth, repelled by the Moon's sky, are those that were "during their life wholly distracted by passions" (*On the Sign of Socrates*, 591d); the souls that manage to escape from the rising tide of the Styx, instead, have learned to preserve the proper ties with their part "left free from corruption," which "is called by the multitude the understanding [Nous], who take it to be within themselves . . . but those who conceive the matter rightly call it a demon [Daimon], as being external" (591e). These souls *stand* firm in relation to their daimon; on hearing its voice they become docile and meek "like a domestic animal," henceforth they recognize their daimon "needing no painful blows" (592c). The soteriological emphasis of Plutarch's demonology therefore does not change the fundamental trait of Plato's demon: the exteriority of the daimon and the necessary custody it exercises over the soul that has fallen into the body. To this end, the distinction between Nous and Daimon is essential: the soul cannot save itself by itself, *kyklou te lexai* (Proclus, *In Timaeum*, 42c–d) and "catch its breath from misery" (as Colli translates Orpheus, fr. 229 Kern), without encouragement and aid from the daimon. But the daimon's voice will never be discordant with what the soul has decided, as witnessed by the Moirai.

If the daimon maintains a separate essence, it is difficult to imagine it otherwise than as a function or minister of Anangkē (necessity). If, on the other hand, the daimon is identified with the human soul or, more precisely, with the *superhegemonic* faculty of the soul (this clearly occurs in Plotinus: *Enneads*, III, 4), the Nous that is free in us becomes the decisive factor thanks to which we can move towards a demonic or even a divine life (III, 4, 3). Nous versus Anangkē—but then every essential distinction between demon and soul disappears. Here is defined *the* problem in the relationship between classical demonology and angelology: two contradictory requirements are supposed to be fulfilled by the Angel—it has a nature separate from the soul, from consciousness, and from Nous, yet it is also free from the law of Anangkē. The Angel intercedes, rescues, and helps in ways incomparable to those of Plutarch's demon: the Angel induces humans to correct and overcome that to which they seem to be destined; the Angel participates in the soul's reckless struggle to free itself from the bind of Anangkē.[33] The *root* of the Angel is opposed to that of the daimon; their difference does not involve so much the character or the functions that both exercise: the demon may turn out terrible or happy, bonus or malus Eventus, a genius that cares after the birth and vis procreativa (procreative force) of human beings or a genius of destruction and revenge. The daimon may appear in the pitiful guise of Thanatos and Hypnos, which lay our bodies in the grave, or in the guise of furious Erinyes. Each species of demon, each power dwells between the divine and the human, and we breathe it in with our very breathing[34]—just as there are infinite types of Angels, from the highest ones to those fallen into the lowest circles of the chasm of Hades. The difference is radical—and no simple phenomenology can do justice to it. The difference regards the *root* of the daimon, which is the same as daiomai, dainymi: to distribute, to cast lots. This root[35] inexorably assigns the daimon to the empire of the Moirai.[36] And our *ethos* cannot disentangle itself from the daimon. The Angel, instead, not only safeguards, but also induces and e-ducates; it wants to transform and transfigure, assuming a unique eschatological dimension extraneous to the daimon. Yet more important, the Angel induces the soul to break free of its own demonic part, to accomplish the *miracle* of freeing itself from the demon of Necessity. Round after round of the Wheel, the demon constrains the soul to the *part* it has chosen for itself; the Angel wants the soul to contradict it, *down here*. The demon *endures* "on the ropes": it depends on the bind, the thread, the cosmic network. This is the double situation of the daimon: it is bound to the primordial ground, closer to the Urgrund than any of the angelic figures, and yet enchained and predestined, a mere prisoner. The *rope* that enchains the universe, like the undergirders of triremes (*Republic*, X, 616 b–c), grips the demon in its own light and transforms it into a *puppet* (Mircea Eliade has brilliantly explained this symbolism on many occasions). The destiny of the daimon is the puppet, *not* the doll of Rilke which educates to "that tremendous silence (larger than life) which was later to come to us repeatedly out of space, whenever we approached the frontiers of our existence at any point" (Rilke, *Puppen*, English trans., p. 46), and *against* such a destiny the Angel is called to lead an interminable struggle.

This explains why in the eyes of angelology every demon is "evil"; this is why all pagan gods (all of them much weaker than Anangkē) "become" daimones, "evil" daimones. Origen finds no difficulty, in his polemic against Celsus, in attributing to Angels many of the functions that pagan religiosity attributes to the demons because, as we saw, this does not affect the radical difference: these functions are carried out by the daimon within the context of the law of Adrastea—but the Angel uses them to e-ducate man, to convince him of what appears, according to Necessity, impossible; convince him to hope against all hope. The figures of demons, compelled to insuperable *metra*, finally coincide with the signs of the stars, while the angelic intelligence is pure Nous, the eighth Heaven beyond the sphere of planets. This is the itinerary of Gnostic angelology (particularly in its theurgical aspects), but also, in its fundamental inspiration, that of Neoplatonic demonology, from Plotinus to Proclus. In the latter, though, the daimon is no longer a term that indicates a separate essence: the demon does not hide in the intimacy of the soul, but *is* the intimacy of the soul, the active and hegemonic faculty of the soul, its inexhaustible life. In accordance with its form of life, the soul continuously elects its own demon: it is demon to itself. The ethos is not a demon in the sense of a power that commands and determines, but the ethos is its own demon: we choose our demon in accordance with our way of acting, behaving, and living; that is, the soul shows which of *its* powers has hegemony in it. But here there is no place for the Angel as such. It becomes another name for the force and power of the soul. No doubt this is only partially true because, as we saw, there exist "separate substances" to which Proclus attributes an actual creative power. This in turn will be refuted by Christian angelology (see Thomas Aquinas, *De Substantiis Separatis*, c.10), for which the Angel guides and enlightens, and only in this restricted sense can it be said to have a causal efficacy. Is a different outcome conceivable? In the struggle against the demon, does one not necessarily end up denying a place to the Angel itself? How can one maintain the separateness of the Angel, where it expresses the "free" power of Nous? If the Angel inherits the "freedom" of Nous, how can it be imagined separate from the soul, having its own figure and filling a specific "part"? In the theodrama dominated by Anangkē the role of the demon was clear. But what "necessity" does the Angel preserve if it is free from Necessity? Are not all of its functions already interiorized in the itinerary of the soul? Are they not all already remembered by heart? is not the Angel, in Rilke's words, already part of the universal "gedeutete Welt," of the "interpreted" world?

Ou-topia of the Angel—neither demon, nor simple faculty of the soul; radically akin to humans in itinere (in itinerary), it thinks the impossible (to be free from Anangkē) and yet is still inextricably connected (for all the reasons already considered and for others that we will see) to the world of the metaxy animated by innumerable spirits subject to the Moirai. The Angel has no proper place, but *for this reason* it is the "necessary" figure of the instant that brings to a standstill the arrow of time, that interrupts the continuum. Placeless Angel, *hence* the "necessary" companion of Tobias—young, young *to the point of infancy* that no discourse can explain or resolve. This is how Klee imagines the New Angel: irrevocable only in that it has been once, has sung for *an instant*. This instant is the catastrophe of every solid continuum.[37] This instant produces an Openness without closure, which cannot be filled or repeated—free from the cycle of rebirths. The empty-handed freedom of this "poor" instant is granted to us. We are still e-ducated to it by the last Angel, the oldest and the youngest of them all: the New Angel.

The New Angel is free, but without a trace of gnostic hubris. Definitely young, yet not perfectly *Renatus* (re-born). Mixed with its puerile traits are words of profound disenchantment and the distance of a self-dissolving irony. Its figure resembles that of a *young Melancholia*. When we finally apprehend their rustling and, as if by miracle, seize their undivided time, the New Angels *seem* to be "the most joyous creatures in the world" (G. Leopardi, *In Praise of Birds*).[38] Their existence seems to be song, laughter, and flight. And just as the ancient sages deemed that the air was populated by demons, now these "vocal and musical creatures" inhabit it. The images of Leopardi remind us of the most "joyful" ones in the angelological tradition, from Pseudo-Dionysius to Dante: the *aeikinesia* ("[they] remain in the same place for a very short while": it is the Plotinian psyche, eternal principle of motion); the incessant change of place (ubiquity of the angelic creature—a central theme, as we have already seen in Swedenborg); their perfect sight and hearing ("In flying it sees and sings", *Paradiso*, XXX, 4–6); laughter as their proper form of expression (they do not speak nor really sing, but they *laugh*). They are like children who know nothing of boredom, endowed with a fervid, light, and unstable imagination that the profound and tumultous imagination proper to adult Melancholia seems unable to ravish. Nonetheless, the "catastrophic present" of linguistic maturity, that "origin of most grievous and perpetual anxiety and anguish" that befalls the "pleasant and joyful thoughts" and the "sweet illusions" of children, is not simply *other* with respect to the figure of the Angel, the Bird of the soul. It would be too simple, and at the end reassuring, to see in this relation an absolute, immediate opposition. The laughter of the New Angel, which forcefully seems to deliver it from the time of succession, from causal relations, from necessity and boredom, also belongs to man—to the elderly, to those that are both civilized and without hope. The more his life becomes miserable and tormented, the more man laughs. "I would think that the first occasion and the first cause for men to laugh was drunkenness." There is no truth in wine except for the interruption of pain, "the interval, so to speak, of life": the *instant*, the most fleeting of instants, when humans are granted laughter and song. One is reminded of the extraordinary page in Plato where the chorus of elders, of the fathers and sages of the polis, is chosen to address a drunken song to Dionysus (Plato, *Laws*, II, 665–666).

A profound and intimate *sympathy* connects the laughter of this elder, who suspends for an instant the terrible pain of old age with the pharmakon (drug) of wine, to the "laughing eyes," the "perpetual song" of the Angel-bird (this is why Sylvia laughs and sings *an instant*, and *in this instant* dwells perpetually). The New Angels "linger but for a brief moment": they, too, become old, drunk; their laughter confounds itself with this song, their song with this laughter. *If* Angels and the elders were to testify to the happiness of things, their testimony would be *false*. But is that what they say or show? Do they not rather show their tie, the complexio (dilemma) that unites them *as opposites*? Are they not rather witness of this: the infinitely poor, "empty-handed" freedom that shatters Necessity is nothing but an instant—*and yet it is*—as desperate and disenchanted as the feast of the old Athenians and *at the same time* joyous, light as a child, ungraspable as the one of Tobias and his Birds?

Wretched Angel, fragmented Angel, Angel interiorized in the passion of the soul, fallen Angel—Angels suspended between "the two worlds of feeling" (the exactness and certainty of Swedenborg, who spoke with them "as if they were inhabitants of Stockholm," and the self-concentration into "pure silence" on whose breath Musil's novel takes leave)—Angels caught in a world where "a murder may appear to us as a crime or as an heroic deed, and the hour of love as a feather that has fallen from an angel's wing or one from the wing of a goose" (R. Musil, *The Man Without Qualities*, vol. 1, trans. E. Wilkins and E. Kaiser [New York: Capricorn Books, 1965], p. 297)—the contemporary iconology of the Angel turns upon these themes.[39] "Adónde el Paraíso, / sombra, tú que has estado? / Pregunta con silencio" ("Where's Paradise, shadow, / you who have been there? / A question in silence") (R. Alberti, "Paraíso perdido," in *Sobre los ángeles*. English trans., "Paradise Lost," in *Concerning the Angels*, trans. G. Connell [London, 1967]). Paradise is lost *when it is looked for*, but the search continues "sin luz para siempre" ("stripped of light, for ever"). Good and bad angels, unknown and nameless angels, languishing angels, spirits that confound their ancient attributes with incomprehensible hybridizations, dead angels swarm in the mystery that embraces the word, as sign of the realissimum that no word can grasp or denote. They flood our everyday life;[40] their abode is inseparable from the *air* one breaths: "they have hurled you into my soul" ("Eviction"). They must be found—they *ask* to be found—in those "puddles which cannot hold a cloud," "in the dented desertions endured by worn-out furniture," "under the drop of wax that buries a word in a book," near "an open razor left lying at the edge of a precipice" ("The Dead Angels"). This is the defeat of Heaven—stunned and confused, Angels fall down here, in our soul, in its names, because our soul, too, invokes them, invokes the invisible whose wounded testimony they are. That defeat, then, is not a sim-

ple kenosis. If the Angels are no longer solidly fixed to their heavenly places, if the "Waltzes of Heaven" no longer hold them, the
reason is that they have been able to break every "religio" with
Necessity. Their clipped wings[41] are the price paid for the freedom
of their instant from the power of the demon, their freedom from
the continuous dis-course of words and presences. Now we have to
look for them everywhere and nowhere; no "method" or magic
knows how to evoke and grasp them.[42] They preserve what is
ungraspable *by* presence and discourse: this is the content of the
letter that "an angel brought down from heaven" ("The Good
Angel").

The letter is delivered to the poet, to whom God grants "la
souffrance / Comme un divin remède" ("suffering / As the only
divine remedy") (Baudelaire, *Bénédiction*. English trans., *The
Blessing*, in *Flowers of Evil*), and the nobility of sorrow "où ne mor-
dront jamais la terre et les enfers" ("on which neither earth nor
Hell can lay its fangs"). An *invisible* Angel protects the poet in this
work of transfiguration and metamorphosis of pain into the fra-
grance of ambrosia and nectar, into laetitia (joy), into the pure
light of which mortal eyes "ne sont que des miroirs obscurcis et
plaintifs" ("are no more than dimmed and mortal mirrors"). Thus
the Angel in *Mort des Amants* revives, "fidèle et joyeux" ("faithful
and joyful"), the tarnished mirrors and dead flames; it commands
the withered heart to love the Beautiful (*Que diras-tu ce soir, pau-
vre âme solitaire* ["What shall you say tonight, poor soul so full of
care"]); it reawakens the tormented ideal, the phantasm of the
shining soul, equal to the immortal sun (*L'aube spirituelle*). The
metaphysical detachment of *Réversibilité* has to be understood as
the origin of this questioning, of this search; it has value not as a
quieted result, but as the first moment of an uncertain and difficult
philia (friendship) in which the image of the Angel corresponds to
the poet's gaze into the invisible.[43] The detachment is the mutual
reflection between the Angel that is by now a-topos (without place)
and "la honte, les remords, les sanglots, les ennuis" ("the shame
and remorses, sobs and cares") that oppress the heart of man—it is
the *mirror* that divides and at the same time gives way. This is why
the Angel—and above all the New Angel—masters the art of glass-
making. The mirror returns to us without pity the image of our
transience ("look into a mirror for all your life and you will see

Death at work as bees in a glass beehive" says the glassmaker Angel Heurtebise to Orpheus),[44] but it is always also a sign, which constitutes itself for what is Other (not this or that entity, but the Other in general, that is, what lies "behind" the mirror). The transience of the image reflected in the mirror is metaphysically separated and, at the same time, inextricably connected to the permanence of this Other. Death comes and goes through mirrors, which are the "craft" of the Angel. Death is what permanently gives itself in the image, the unalterable presupposition of everything that the mirror reflects. And the New Angel reflects itself with us in this mirror, the last of the heavenly mirrors, the only one it was able to bring down from Heaven after it was hurled into our soul.

The New Angel resembles a new Narcissus.[45] Like the Ancient Flower, it comes with the mirror. While the great Angels of old time speculated on the "eternal value," the New Angel loves the infinite names of the risked, doubtful, incomplete and ephemeral image reflected in the mirror of Heurtebise. "A kind of angel was seated upon the rim of a well. He looked for his reflection and found that he was a Man, and in tears . . . prey to an infinite sorrow" (P. Valéry, *The Angel*).[46] The figures *of* mirrors, in the "solid and dead water of crystal," in fact seem "incredibly alien and distant."[47] But, running into their phantasm, the Angel is forced to return to the state of the hermetic Anthropos—or, rather, reflecting and meditating on itself in the mirror of water, it becomes Anthropos. But now it could no longer fall in love with this image. The image makes it despair: how did it happen that from being perfect knowledge, reflection of the Light, and Flower of the soul, the Angel could fall down to this "station" that stands at the origin of all human misery? Unlike man, the Angel cannot even hope for an answer, because all questioning is contradictory with respect to its nature. Its essence could never give a reason for the pain it now has to suffer. "Is there then something other than light?" Slowly, it is forced to discover this by looking us over, reflecting its image in us or, better, reflecting itself with us in *one* source. The Angel recognizes that other things exist apart from light, *no longer* recognizing its own image in this mirror. Up there, its mirrors were not traversed by Death. Faced with an image of itself that it cannot say, the Angel becomes infant. The unsurpassable dimension of man's in-fancy[48] attracts and confounds it, like the current does with

Narcissus. The Angel could surrender to this dimension—but it can also correspond to it with tense and attentive *melancholia*. The latter is the case of the New Angel: called upon to question the instant, problem of representation posed by Baudelaire's "phantasm," knowledge that does not comprehend ("he never ceased to know and fail to understand" says Valéry of his Angel-Narcissus), that does not possess, grasp, dispose—*it* is safeguarded in the gaze into the invisible of the word.[49] The word is that mirror: it reflects the transient image with which it will never be able to identify, in the very moment that it *is sign* (sēmainein—neither saying, nor hiding) of the Other that is irreducible to the image itself and that every image presupposes.

3

THE PROBLEM OF REPRESENTATION

Only the Angel, free from demonic destiny, poses the problem of representation. Demonic destiny is "der Schuldzusammenhang des Lebendigen" (W. Benjamin, *Schicksal und Charakter*),[1] the guilt context of the living. For the demon, the constitution of the living is guilty: it refers back to an originary guilt that condemned to the first incarnation and set in motion the rota generationis (cycle of rebirths). Life itself is the penalty. The daimon nails life to the laws of destiny, which have nothing in common with those of justice.[2] The dimension of the daimon thus absorbs that of character: character "abdicates itself in favor of the guilty life."[3] But, at bottom, this also occurs in Plato: having chosen its own life, the soul is constrained in it by the daimon. Ethos becomes a demon for man, which he cannot escape except through a new death and a new birth.

Benjamin intends to break the chain that connects the concept of character to that of destiny. Knowledge has always interwoven a tight net in which these two concepts become indistinguishable wefts—and because of which every character can be judged in light of an immutable Law, according to Right. Character becomes a daimon subject to destiny. In this context a *problem* of representation cannot exist because the character *is* the daimon and the daimon *is* the power of that destiny. In the texture that ties these terms, no questions or holes are left open. And yet, for Benjamin, tragedy has already cut through the texture. "Heimlich," secretly, pagan man here tries to summon his own strength; at this time begins his victory against the demons. In the last letter of the *Philosophische Briefe*, Schelling had already said that "Greek tragedy honored human freedom because it made the hero *struggle* against the superior force of destiny." Guilt and punishment are shaken together and confused by the tragic poet; each Nomos has another opposing it, each Logos a counterpoint. The discourses of tragedy appear to be *dissoi*, double, and extremely *dissoi* are those of the god, servant-custodian of Anangkē. But even if this knowledge strips man of words, reduces him to silence, and seemingly annihilates him, it is here that "for the first time the head of genius lifted itself from the mist of guilt" and felt essentially free from demonic destiny. It is true that the hero must succumb, but because he succumbs *not* without struggling, he demonstrates by his own downfall, through the very loss of his freedom, that in the downfall lies "precisely this freedom": he perishes "with an open affirmation (Erklärung) of free will" (F. W. J. Schelling, *Philosophie der Kunst*).[4] The adventure of his autonomous logos also begins from here. In comedy, character "unfolds radiantly" and lets nothing exist by its side; comedy affirms the freedom and autonomy of character from the daimon. The comic persona, far from being the "puppet of determinists," opposes "the brilliance of its single trait" to the closely woven texture of Destiny. To the primacy of guilt it opposes "a vision of the natural innocence of man." The comic persona *plays* with the demonic character precisely by defining with lucid consequentiality its own irreducible individuality.

But such autonomy presupposes that of the logos that is the form of expression proper to the comic persona. Its freedom, as Benjamin perceives it without further developing the problem, affirms itself by way of its affinity to logic ("auf dem Wege ihrer Affinität mit der Logik"). The tragic word knows nothing of this affinity; since it shakes together and confuses guilt and atonement, it cannot follow the criteria of logic. This word does not represent but rather *reverberates* a sound whose origin is concealed, an *adēlon*, something inscrutable.[5] The tragic word cannot proclaim an autonomy with regard to this *adēlon*. Autonomous, instead, is the logic of the comic character who ceases to be simply a "knot in the net" (Benjamin) to become an *individuum* who unfolds himself on the basis of the uniqueness of *his* fundamental trait or *temperament*. The discourse of this individual becomes substance unto itself, complementary to nothing and corresponding only to its internal order. The "comic" aims at the annihilation of all reality external to the unfolding of character: from the perspective of the concept of destiny and of daimon, it is the acme of hubris and arrogance.

Hence the problem of representation, which began already with the tragic form, bursts open. What is the relation between an autonomous logic (no longer reverberation, resonance, medium) and the thing? In what way can a logos that is metaphysically detached from every presupposition represent a thing that is different and heterogeneous from it? How can the logoi stand for the thing itself if no common origin is expressible; if the logos, in breaking the net of demonic destiny, has defined itself absolutely or autonomously? In tragedy, a logos that already doubts of all solid, transcendent foundations is still tormented by their idea, and to attain it goes down to the ground, founders,* in this desperate search. In comedy, precisely the judiciousness of this search is criticized: the character is not a demon, but every demonic dimension is here completely subsumed under the individuality of character so that the appearance, manifestation, and expression of this character is everything. But this expression can only be that of the *onomazein* (to name), of the *onoma*, of the mere name "that mortals posited convinced that it is true" (Parmenides, 8, 39 DK; English trans., L. Tarán, *Parmenides* [Princeton, N.J.: Princeton University Press, 1965]). The name reflects the doxai, the opinions of mortals, the deceiving order, the apparent disposition of the world. The name is the arbitrary instrument of humans "eidotes ouden," who know nothing, "dikranoi," double-headed, whose amēchaniē guides into the hearts the plakton noon, whose helplessness guides their wandering thought (Parmenides, 6 DK). If logos scours the path "for which being and non-being is the same and not the same," if it renounces the absoluteness of alētheia (unconcealment), if it erects itself in auto-nomy with respect to the unbeatable force of Necessity, then it necessarily resolves itself into the onomazein. But one cannot make the onoma correspond to a certain and stable being. The onoma is nothing but the representation of the oscillation of the entity in the doxa of mortals. Properly speaking, it represents only the deceiving order of this same doxa in its perennial change of place and color.

How can one represent that which is absolutely opposed to the untrembling heart of Alētheia? How can one know that which never persists? And how is it possible for the arbitrarily posited and perennially changing name to contain *one* representation of anything? The truly real thing, on principle, escapes the realm of opinion to which the name belongs. No name "has a bit of stability because nothing prevents things that are now round to be called straight, and things straight to be called round" (Plato, *Seventh Letter*, 343 a–b; trans. L.A. Post [Princeton, N.J.: Princeton University Press, 1985]). Name, definition, and image form the obscure and unstable knowledge of the oscillating entity that has nothing to do with the "fifth," superior level of knowledge corresponding to the truly real thing. And if anyone were to affirm that the onomazein can comprehend the "fifth," then this person would certainly be afflicted by the madness of mortals and not struck by the *mania* that comes from the gods.

But not only does the abyss of the truly real thing escape the name, not only does the essential *no-thingness* of Being evade that knowledge which is an ephemeral order of opinion constructed by names, definitions, and images—even the *on* (being) that is looked for in the onoma (so Plato explains the term in the *Cratylus*: "on ou masma estin" ["being is that of which there is a search"], 421 a–b) will never be effectively drawn out from the onoma. The search that the name conducts is in principle interminable. If, indeed, the image were a perfect imitation, if the name perfectly stood for the thing, then one would not speak of a name or an image but rather of a duplication of the *on* itself. "Do you not perceive that images are very far from having qualities which are the exact counterparts of the realities which they represent? . . . But then how ridiculous would be the effect of names on things, if they were exactly the same with them! For they would be the doubles of them, and no one would be able to determine which were the names and which were the realities" (*Cratylus* 432d; trans. Benjamin Jowett [Princeton, N.J.: Princeton University Press, 1985]). Whoever knows the names therefore does not know the things, neither in the sense of knowing the "thing itself" (439d), the truth of the thing (438e), nor in the sense of a perfect adherence to the appearance of the entity, a complete *touching*, point by point, of the *on*, in short, a complete re-presentation of it. How can names signify the truth of the thing if they appear intrinsically ambiguous, if they are not in agreement between themselves, if the legislators who posited them could not dispose of other names from which to learn (and thus could not have learned the "thing itself" of the *on* through the name)? Is it wise for a man to "put himself or the education of his mind in the power of names" (440c), if the knowledge that comes from them is ever-changing and thus will always be *unknowing*?

The break with the demonic character seals the fate of this questioning: it becomes *Socratic* comedy. Comedy is the infinite variation of this one question: if representation by means of the name does not give the thing but the doxa about the thing, how will it be possible to draw out knowledge of the thing by way of the things themselves? How can one learn the truth of the thing in itself, the truth that is always intuitable by a knower who also always is? The liberation of character from the daimon coincides with the liberation of the name from being the signified, that is, from being the imitation-image of the thing that it signifies. The name unfolds "in the brilliance of its single trait" (Benjamin), in the solitude of its "temperament." The character "freely" wanders through names and their etyma, combining and varying them in a game of intelligence and invention that challenges the original resonance of the word: you are not persuaded by this meaning? you think this explanation is coarse?—then see if this other one satisfies you (399e). Çan we really question ourselves *seriously* on the reason of names? "The serious explanation is not to be had from me, but there is no objection to your hearing the facetious one; for the gods too love a joke" (406c). It is all a *joke*, then, that Dionysus is the one who gives wine, that Aphrodite means born of foam, that Pallas-Athena is the earthshaker. The onomazein does not "touch" the truth; it is impossible to learn the thing itself through names. The divine is not its names (it is practically a mockery ante-litteram of Usener's *Götternamen*). But it is precisely the "joke" of the name, or of the care for the name (which already cast its shadow in tragic drama) that undermines the dominion of the daimon over character. The "joke" of the *Cratylus* therefore appears to be terribly serious. It is the question that Socrates continually repeats to himself "as if in a dream": how can one represent and learn the "thing itself" that we have under consideration not when we observe a beautiful face in its flowing and not-being, but the beautiful always just as it is? How can one represent the idea if it cannot be apprehended through the kaleidoscopic game of the onomazein?

This problem constitutes that "Angel with the flaming sword of the concept" which Scholem sees erected at the entrance of the "paradise" of the written work—the "Epistemo-critical Prologue" of *The Origin of German Tragic Drama*.[6] But the Angel safeguards the whole of Benjamin's oeuvre: an oeuvre that is marked by the confrontation with the Platonic problem of representation, which is devastating for the demonic character constrained by the chains of Necessity. At every turning point in time, at every *krisis*, "mit jeder Wendung," philosophical literature must return to the "Frage der Darstellung" (question of representation). If the reflection of "normal time" forgets or leaves no room for the consideration (Rücksicht) of representation, then the philosophy of the time of krisis, or better, of time as *krisis*, assumes as its own essential task the re-garding, the returning to meditate on the question of representation. The time of crisis coincides with the time of the return—of the anamnesis—of philosophy as the question of representation.

The representation in question is that of the idea. Benjamin affirms this explicitly: "If representation is to stake its claim as the real methodology of the philosophical treatise, then it must be the representation of ideas." But the idea, insofar as it is the "property" of consciousness, cannot be a pro-duct of the intellect's spontaneity; names are the properties and pro-ducts of consciousness. The idea must be considered as "ein Vorgegebenes," something pre-given to consciousness. The struggle for representation is renewed at every *crisis*: either when the dimension of the idea as a "Vorgegebenes" risks becoming the prey of a negative theology (for which there is no possible representation of the idea) or—but the two aspects can be closely intertwined—when it is presumed that the idea can be represented by names-definitions-images. When this risk is greatest, then the struggle for representation, as representation of ideas, "eternal constellations" undetermined by intention, is renewed.

The being of the idea is a-intentional, distinct from the connection proper to knowledge, and "exempt from mediation." The idea is not the eidos, or form of observation; it is not a form of vision. Benjamin explicitly rejects the neo-Kantian interpretation of Plato. The idea whose representation poses the problem here is not the eidos that in-forms representation. The problem consists in the representational giving of itself of the idea, and not of the forms with which a "civilization of vision" represents the idea to itself. "Truth is the death of intention"; any theory that wants to reduce truth to the ambit of the intentional relation is destined to miss "the peculiar giving of itself of truth from which any kind of intention remains withdrawn." The forms of the analytic-conceptual connection presume to represent truth just as names presume to possess in themselves the thing itself. In reality, this conception betrays only an ignorance of the problem of representation. If representation stands for the identical image of the thing, we return to the aporia of the "double" in the *Cratylus*. We would then have to say that the forms of the connection are truth itself. But these forms are made up of names and verbs; they form the world of the experience of the entity in its oscillation. That is why they must be rigorously differentiated from the forms in which truth gives itself. If we were to pro-duce these forms, truth would be the pro-duct of our intention; but our intention, again, cannot develop itself except through names and verbs. That is why the problem of representation can be understood only as the problem of the giving-itself on its own of truth itself.

A philosophy that corresponds to this problem does not find itself in the condition of mere "research" to which a "current conception" reduces or even subordinates it.[7] The researcher moves in the sphere of the simple "extinction of the empirical" or of the "negative polemic." His art of confutation shows only the imperfect nature of the "four" levels and the unattainability of the "fifth" by means of the knowledge that finds its origin in the name. The researcher is an ironist whose art "extinguishes" the empirical by showing the constitutive instability of its names, its *not*-being-ever. But this art does not confront the problem of representation and so limits itself to a negative polemic. The philosopher, instead, questions himself about the *positive* representation of the idea. Philosophy certainly pertains, on one side, to research since it is also vitally interested in the "extinction of the empirical," but it distinguishes itself from research because amid the fever of the negative that seizes definitions and images to submit them to a meticulous skepsis, amid the toil and effort aimed at removing the dimension of opinion and naming, philosophy remains attentive to the splendor, the gleaming of truth in its a-intentional essence. One should note that for Benjamin this means the exact opposite of an ek-static intuition of truth; here it is not a question of "ascending" to a superior vision through some initiatory itinerary.[8] Truth *gives itself* simply, haplōs, not mediated by our faculty of representation, but as if suddenly intuited (for Plato intuition is the faculty closest to the "fifth"). This giving of itself is that of the thing—but of the thing itself, of the itself of the thing, which is in principle irreducible to the net of connections represented by naming-defining. Truth gives itself immediately as the thing itself, and cannot be questioned further as to its ground or reason. The "fifth" intuits the realissimum that can only give itself, and it gives itself precisely by withdrawing from every definition. Naming grasps not the realissimum but the functions, connections, and entities that are conceivable only in their mutual relations. This is why each name collects in itself some portion of the other names (being understood only in their context: *Seventh Letter*, 343a). The name is intrinsically a mediation with its other. But the thing itself slips through the meshes of the net of definition, shines in every definition as the *that which this is* that always withdraws from it and gives itself as the definition's own undefinable. That which is in, yet withdraws from, the definition is not at all an absolutely transcendent dimension but, rather, is precisely the thing itself, *just* the thing, the this-here individuum of the thing.

The *thing* must be said to the Angel. Precisely the *thing itself*, "invisible" to the functional definition, must be brought to the invisible Angel, to the Invisible that is the non-place of the Angel. But how will it be *said*? Is there a way of saying things that is extricable from the onomazein? Is there a word wherein that truth which has the pure and simple, haplōs, consistency of the thing may give itself? Benjamin's "Prologue" turns upon this question. For Benjamin, the name that "determines the givenness of ideas" cannot be understood as a form of the onomazein; it must appear, so to speak, *after* the Platonic critique. In Benjamin, the name excludes any "explicit profane meaning"; it determines the giving of itself of the idea only insofar as a *symbolic* dimension belongs to it—that is, only insofar as the idea attains *self-transparency* in the name. The thing itself and the name consequently form a symbol. One must listen to the name resonate by itself, as "it itself," *at one* with the thing. One must listen to the name not insofar as it *serves* the definition of the thing in the network of its relations, but as the sound of the thing itself, *one* with the giving of itself of the thing. Just as naming functions in the representation of the relationships between entities in their flowing, so also the name can appear as symbol of the thing itself, a-intentional self-transparency of the thing itself.

Through us, the most ephemeral, the name-symbol speaks to the Angel. The name, in which the thing "saves" itself in its in itself, communicates with the Angel, with that dimension which is unattainable by the onomazein. One communicates with the Angel through the *intransitivity* of the name.[9] If an intransitive dimension of the name *gives itself*, so that the name resonates as the thing itself, without reason or aim, then the idea is representable. For Benjamin, philosophy is essentially the uninterrupted struggle for the restoration of the "primacy" of the symbolic, for the creation of a space for the name as symbol, because only in the name-symbol does the idea give itself. The "Frage der Darstellung" becomes the problem of the name in its abstraction from the onomazein, of the intransitivity of the name, which *thenceforth* is symbol of the thing itself, *thenceforth* determines the giving of itself of the idea. The task of the philosopher proceeds under the sign of Eros: Eros for the proper representation of the name-symbol. Eros for saying the thing itself to the Angel through the "intact nobility" of the intransitive word. *To say the thing* is (would be) already saying to the Angel because to say the thing is (would be) to say that realissimum that cannot be said through the onomazein (in which subject and object remain separated), but only through a name that is symbol of the thing—self-transparency of the thing itself as such, "saved," that is, as idea. The name-symbol of the thing that stands "saved at last," as "a thing that is" (*Seventh Elegy*, 69–71), this *idea* of the thing has to be recovered, "erected," in the gaze of the Angel—there one needs to listen for the sound of the word still living: House, Bridge, Fountain, Door, Window, Tree, Tower, Column. One needs to say them *in this way* as none of "these" things, captured in the net of discoursing, has ever in its intimacy imagined itself to be. One needs to say each of them as an individual idea; better, to let them shine through in the symbolic dimension of the word that even in the "streets of the City of Sorrow" (Leid-Stadt) (*Tenth Elegy*, 16) still withstands intact by itself.

The name-symbol does not possess the thing but represents its giving of itself. Those words that Rilke pronounces have the *consistency* of things; they are not the thing, but like the thing itself. The Angel does not orient man to the conquest of the unrevealable but to the recognition of its self-transparency in Eros, of which this "like" is the sole manifestation. And even the Angel, as we know, is not the hermeneut of the highest Point but rather the patient exegete of its infinite names. The pathos that moves man toward the name-symbol is therefore shared by the Angel. Its figure resembles more that of a companion caught in our own vicissitudes than that of the hermetic-gnostic Psychopomp. The Angel *follows* man; it desires to be named by man's desire for the name. The New Angel of Benjamin is the last figure of the tradition, delineated in the preceding chapters, in which the Angel ends up inextricably implicated in *all* the dimensions of our saying, of our possible sayings. And this is why it appears to have an increasing affinity with their *catastrophes*, turned toward them, *entwined* in them. *Angel* it remains, all the same. Even if it flashes always new in the instant, the Angel is the form of the giving of itself, in the time of the Leid-Stadt, of the idea in the name. And such representation of the idea, because it means the Platonic "saving" of phenomena, also preserves the messianic-eschatological theme proper to the sound of the Angel (which we will develop later). Twisted around toward our allegorical dimension (our Trauerspiel) to the point of sharing in our fallenness, the Angel nevertheless does not lose the guiding thread of the problem of representation. And only then, we may conclude, does the allegorical game become authentic Mourning (Trauer): once it takes to heart the problem of representation, once it searches, in the Angel, for the symbolical dimension of the name—and *here*, in this search, in this attempting-to-say, disregarding easier moorings, it shipwrecks.

But of what idea is the Angel the proper exegete? The idea that represents itself in the name of the Angel will have to express the proper eschatological value of any representation. The Angel, in fact, is an exegete precisely in this sense: it lets phenomena *emerge* from their appearance, from out of the slavery of the letter, diverting them from their immediate presence to re-present them according to their truth, finally doing them *justice*. Whereas the hermeneutical exercise renders *right* to propositions, orders their connections according to right, and so *judges* them, the exegesis of the Angel renders justice-*praise* to the symbolical dimension of the name. But this Angel is the New Angel, turned to the ephemeral: how will its figure really make it so that the thing "returns," as a point, in the eternal constellation of ideas? Of what idea can the Angel, as the New Angel, be the exegete?

In the so-called esoteric fragment of Ibiza, *Agesilaus Santander*, the Angel's song (which chants the *Eternal*) represents by *dividing*. Its exegesis begins by examining and *accusing*; it makes one feel distress, *penia* (need), for the absence of the loved one. But it is as if this principle of separation were projected against the background of that song and then, from its interior, ripened an incoercible power to wait, an invincible patience.[10] Accusing and separating, the Angel e-ducates to the wait and the patience for the name. The wings of the Angel are the wings of this patience, of this prosochē or attention to the symbolic dimension of the name that always gives itself and that is neither an absolutely separate-transcendent dimension nor an unfathomable mythos (better, that *adēlon* more originary than every mythein), but the symbolic "primacy" of the word, of *this* word: House and Fountain, Door and Window and Bridge. There is only separation—in the Angel—*together with* this profane attention, with this waiting that draws us to the future through the same movement of remembering (er-innern, ri-cor-dare) the past, because the Angel has sung the Eternal (in the instant, and *thenceforth* it has addressed itself to us, to the ephemeral).

That is how, in the ephemeral, the thing can be "saved" in the name. This "weak messianic force" (Benjamin, *Theses on the Philosophy of History*) granted to us represents itself in the Angel: not pure difference, not difference as separation, but careful and patient exegesis of difference. The New Angel can e-ducate to this exegesis for it is not simply ephemeral but the perfect Ephemeral that has known how to sing-praise the Eternal in the moment. The New Angel safeguards this weak force for us; so that in the ephemeral this may come about. The encounter with the word questioned according to the primacy of the symbol is a fire of exegesis that no exegesis will ever extinguish. But what form can this encounter with the name take in our time, in this time of endless waiting and of *necessary* questioning?

The Angel is the exegete of a dimension of *time* to which a weak messianic force still belongs. The name that is said symbolically between the Angel and us is that of this dimension of time. The problem would not exist if a simple abyss were to gape open between symbol and allegory, or if between them one could establish a "progression" (or a "fall": it amounts to the same), that irreversibly leads from the first to the second. The Angel, however, allegorizes the symbolic as much as it symbolically represents the allegorical. Neither mediator nor pontiff, it names the original symbolic tension that reunites their infinite difference. Angel, but Angel of history—history, but history conceived in the name of the Angel. In this name, history conceived as a continuum, calendar of the always-the-same, permanent passage-transition from present to present, succession of *nyn* (now), ceases to have value. The time of the representation of *ideas* frees itself from the time of "the whore called 'Once upon a time'," the time of the "brothel of historicism," of the Universalgeschichte (universal history) that adds event by event and Erkennen by Erkennen. Not that the Angel (as we already saw) flees ek-statically from the continuum or transcends it, rather the Angel comprehends those events as a "single catastrophe"; it would like to "awaken the dead and recompose what has been shattered"; it maintains a secret understanding with past generations. Breaking the chains of the demonic character is at one with the crisis of time conceived as a relentless succession. Only now is the reason visible for the struggle between Angel and demon, between the weak messianic force and the sovereign argument of invincible Necessity (that if the possible is, it cannot but be real; that possibility is only the potential *of reality*). In the name of the Angel the *idea* becomes self-transparent that it is possible to "blast open" this argument, to blast out of the homogeneous and empty time of the continuum and so give life to days that stand, to Fest-tage (fixed days; holidays) capable of arresting the flow of time and simultaneously recreating it. To entropy and irreversible consumption, the name of the Angel opposes the *ek-tropic* instant. In such a time it is impossible to conceive of an "eternal" image of the past, an image of the past as something that has perfectly been. The past itself is still *in-securus*; it can light up with hope and demand *justice*. In this time the past is never *defeated*; the present is never merely the field of victors from where, as Simone Weil used to say, justice is always forced to retreat.

The Angel incessantly searches for the *just* representation of a *new* time: present-instant, interruption of the continuum, *Jetzt-zeit* (now-time). *Every* Jetzt can represent this new time. The term *Jetzt* has to be read in conjunction with the passage in the *Origin of the German Tragic Drama*, where it is opposed to the mystical-symbolical *Nu*. Still, the Jetzt-zeit does not simply mark the "fall" into the allegorical, but is, in the allegorical, the memory of the symbol. On the strength of this memory the infinite variations of the Spiel (game) transform themselves into a *Trauer*-spiel, a game illuminated precisely by mourning the absence of the symbol. In the Jetzt of the Jetzt-zeit, the time of each "now" is the idea of such a memory. Although weakly, as if in "hesitant immobility," with "a light, imperceptible trembling" the Jetzt-zeit preserves in its name the sole "model of Messianic time" granted to the force with which we are endowed. Moreover, this force represents itself precisely by "saving" the Jetzt-zeit from its profane, immediate meaning, *illu-minating* it without transcending or sublimating it: profane illu-mination. The sole representation of the *eternal* of the idea is given to us in the temporal dimension of the Jetzt-zeit that "exceeds," as instant or moment, mere duration.

It is this same dimension that Rosenzweig comments on with regard to the ending of Psalm 115 (113B); the same dimension of the "conquering *But*"[11] that the living ("But we, the living"), from the depths of their fallenness, can raise in the choral praise of the Living, in the instant of praise, *breaking* with the "scene" domi-nated up to that point by the idolatry of the peoples. The greatest idolatry is the cult of the has-been, of the irredeemable it-was. Against it, the living raise their cry-song to the Living. Only at this point—in the moment of song—can they truly call themselves liv-ing; prior to this they were a succession of moments destined to death, born to die. The living recognize and affirm themselves as living only in the instant, of utmost danger, in which they praise the God who is *not* (the peoples ask "where is" God, but if God belonged in some place it would be only the demon or genius of this place). In this instant, e-ducated by the Angel, they entrust themselves to the Invisible to await its names. The time of this *But*, a fragment detached from the equivalent continuum of nyn, is a cutout:* truly chronos from krinein, tempus from temnein. This dimension of time, held in the cutout (the instant between rock and river of which Rilke says the pure possible), seems to contrast absolutely with that of Aiōn-Aevum-Ewig (eternity), of the unbreachable Hodie (Today), of the Dies (Day) perennial light. But this contraposition is abstract and makes of the eternal an ab-solutum of time; it loses the concrete and living polarity of the two dimensions (just as the abstract separation between the allegorical and the symbolical misses the very idea of the Trauerspiel). Already the great Scholasticism (Jewish, Arab, and Christian) does not limit itself to an opposition between the Nunc stans (standing now) of the divine and the nunc fluens (flowing now) of the creature, but adds a third term: the *Nunc instantis,*[12] the dimension of a *sudden meantime*, so sudden yet so *actual* that it is rarely noticed as a moment of time. A dimension of *perfect* fallenness: the most sudden of moments (fallen like the New Angel) has for its name the instant that arrests and cuts out the continuum. The true name of the most ephemeral, the name of its *idea*, is Nunc instantis. The "tiny door" of which Benjamin talks is an image of this name. Like every door, it unites two sides precisely by separating them: Hodie and nunc fluens, indissoluble polarity, inseparable difference.

The messianic chance, for Benjamin, coincides with the possibilty of representing *this* difference. In Christian theology it tends to be resolved in the triumphant kairos of the Event that is incalculable and unpredictable, yet also full, definitive, *a completed state*. For Benjamin, one cannot "return" from the exile and the separation that irrupted even into the sphere of the divine (so the Angels tell it). But in the *epoch-making* Jetzt-zeit that interrupts and cuts out it is possible to recollect the splinters, sparks, and traces that in the sphere of the creature profanely await redemption; it is possible to brush history against the grain, "die Geschichte gegen den Strich zu bürsten", and so overturn its form of empty duration (be it linear or cyclical); it is possible to discern how the radical incompletion of the world does not necessarily, demonically, produce mere despair over what is shattered, but rather allows to surprise in the thing the sudden meantime of a *Yes* that is stronger than any fall or consumption, of a *But* that ruptures the infinite repetition of the catastrophe. A weak and continually foundering Tikkun,[13] but also one that frees both from the brothels of historicism and from the subtle charm of soothsayers, safeguarding the idea of prophecy from all mythology: not a vision of what is to come, but redemption of *every* moment in its capacity to *name* itself as that instant, that meantime in which the symbolic primacy of the word can represent itself, and do so precisely at the height of the allegorical, amid its ruins. The shadow of this eschatological "reserve" projects itself onto every event, strong enough to free us from every idolatry of what "has been" and every chrono-latry.*[14]

4

ZODIACS

Now we have to retrace our steps. The direction of the gaze of Benjamin's Angel suggests a "cancrizans" (crab-like) movement that Benjamin's own angelology, like that of Rilke and Klee, if analyzed too hastily, can make us forget. In reality, some of the most disturbing aspects of the icon of the Angel have remained in the shadows—precisely those that could best support the provisional conclusion we drew from the polemos between Angel and demon. One has to challenge the overabundance of light in traditional angelology and fix one's sight on its "modesty"; one has to question the seemingly perfect "construct" of its figures, this construct "which never departs from its circles." In the obedience to the cosmos disposed by God, in this Civitas that is a perfect dwelling place, in this mundus imaginalis of the musical hierarchy whose only purpose is the praise of *henosis*, of the creaturely compliance with God by way of its Names—here already gleam signs that darken its splendor; here already one can hear the question posed by Valéry's Angel-Narcissus:[1] "is there then something other than light?" What we may call the kenosis of traditional angelology (but at issue is the far more complex adventure that we have been following) has its prologue in Heaven.

The angelic spirits in postexilic prophetism experienced quite different manifestations than those hierarchies that Pseudo-Dionysius sees "positioned without mediators around God," than the taxis "of the fiery ones" and those who rejoice in "the plenitude of knowledge." At each wheel of the Chariot of the Presence, Ezekiel sees one of four hayoth, living creatures: "each had four faces, and each of them had four wings . . . the soles of their feet were like the sole of a calf's foot; and they sparkled like burnished bronze. Under their wings on their four sides they had human hands. . . . As for the likeness of their faces, each had the face of a man in front; the four had the face of a lion on the right side, the four had the face of an ox on the left side, and the four had the face of an eagle at the back" (Ezekiel 1:5–10). Jewish mysticism has always wanted to see in this tetrad the Angels of the Face, the four Princes of the Presence.[2] God can manifest-represent Himself to man only in an angelical guise (the trinity of Abraham, the Trace that the people follow in the desert), and the order of this manifestation hinges upon these four Angels. The allegorical interpretation of the tetrad, designed to purify it of every "animal" feature, becomes canonized in Maimonides (*Guide of the Perplexed*, III, 1–7). The overall "form" of these beings is human[3] ("they had the likeness of a man"), and their hands were likewise those of a man ("it being known that a man's hands are indubitably formed as they are in order to be engaged in the arts of craftmanship") (Pines trans., p. 417). Only their external features, the external "faces," were of the lion, the bull, and the eagle, for, as Maimonides explains, it is well known "that among men there are some who have faces that resemble those of certain animals"; the proof lies in the Merkabah mysticism in which the figure of the ox is changed for that of the cherub. Therefore all references to animals must be understood in the context of the allegorical language used by the prophets to strike the imagination (see ibid., II, 43). What interests Maimonides is the upward spread of the wings, the forward motion that these beings can maintain while obeying the wind, ruah, that directs them ("Ruah here does not mean wind, but purpose. . . . He [the prophet] says accordingly that the hayoth runs in the direction in which it is the divine purpose that the living creature run") (ibid., III, 2; Pines trans., p. 419), never turning themselves around when going. (This last trait is essential for the understanding of the metaphysical difference between this form of angelic manifestation and that of Benjamin's Angelus Novus).[4]

Jung has pointed out the breadth of the tetrasomatic motif (including its best known derivation, the assignment of one of the features of the hayoth to each of the Evangelists); he has placed *Ezekiel* in relation to the Egyptian image of the four sons of Horus, to the symbolism of the Cross, and through *Daniel* and *Enoch*, to the Gnostic and alchemical developments of the saintly Tetraktys.[5] But the phenomenological analysis must not obscure the essential metaphysical-theological problem raised by this motif: the spiritualization of the "animal" in the theophany of *Ezekiel*, its immediate "metaphorization" into the Angel, occur under the *demonic* sign of necessity—these beings come and go in a flash, instantly obedient to the spirit that directs them. Their figure is enveloped by "a kind of firmament," dominated by the "sapphire stone in the form of a throne." But then why do they have human *hands*? And why insist so much that their figure is distinguished from that of animals? How can this distinction hold if the Angels of Merkabah always move forward, never able to turn around? Maimonides believed that he had prevented any "animal" contamination by pointing to the traditional exchange between the ox and the Cherubim. But the root itself of this term betrays the demonic origin of the Angels of the Face in *Ezekiel*.[6] The tetrad of the Chariot is really composed of Assyrian kāribu, the custodians of Babylonian palaces. Here begins a vicissitude that will leave its mark on the whole of angelology: Babylonian Angels and Archangels[7] "lend" their demonic images to the Neoplatonic ones, to those of the early Christian church, to the Jewish and Christian Gnosis. Idol and Angel, within the same image, indefatigably renew their struggle. The pagan world *lives on* like this, the eternal presupposition that is eternally suppressed and eternally remembered, in the figures and names of the Revelation.[8] The Angel, in virtue of its superior power that is at the same time its fullest creatureliness, concentrates in itself with more profundity this dissension, this "equivocity." Talmudic doctors will try in vain to "purify" its figures through extenuating allegorizations. Orthodox scholasticism will attempt in vain similar actions. The Assyrian kāribu, together with its subsequent Mazdean derivations, with the paganism of the *Chaldean Oracles*, of Porphyry, of Iamblichus, and of the great Gnostic visions all return in the imaginatio of Christianity, Judaism, and Islam. Only by abolishing the Angel as such would it be possible to "cure" it of such images. The cherubim of Pseudo-Dionysius, the Islamic karūbīyūn (Avicenna's intellectual Angels) cannot forget those figures with the head of man and the body of the lion, with the feet of the ox and the wings of the eagle, the powers-archons-daimones of the Babylonian firmament.[9]

The plastic evidence of these images exceeds every measure that is simply allegorical-metaphorical. At the apex of its theophanic function, as Deus revelatus (revealed God) or Logos, the Angel tends to assume animal features. The God-that-reveals-himself is three-quarters animal; its magnificent power, like a "king over all proud beasts" (Job 41:25), terrorizes with its "animal" unpredictability;[10] it reappears in Lamentations 3:10 as the "ursus insidians" ("bear lying in wait") and "leo in absconditis" ("lion in hiding"). (The Gnostic Demiurge at times displays "dangerously" similar features: thus Ialdabaoth in the *Apocryphon of John* is a dragon with lightning eyes.) Angels position themselves around it (forming a *wheel*: the Ofannim of the Chariot in *Ezekiel*) like *zodiacal* signs. Against the background of the fixed firmament dominated by the Throne, the hayoth move looking straight ahead. The *corpora* (bodies) of the zodiac are the *genesis* (beginning) of their spiritual nature: their spirit continuously returns into them and from them it continuously creates itself anew. All of the subsequent zodiacal "placements"[11] of the symbols of the Evangelists and of the figures of the Apostles obey this originary astral-logos. Even the Angels or Archons of darkness must submit to it.[12] The darkness that envelops the world has *twelve* terrifying chambers of torture, and in each one there is an Archon with different features—crocodile, cat, dog, snake, bull, boar (*Pistis Sophia*)[13]—an extraordinary, infernal zodiac that through the most tortuous paths between the Orient and Europe will find its way, represented in its intact violence, into the imaginatio of the late-Gothic up to Bosch; an infernal zodiac whose counterpoint is the heavenly zodiac—but such a balance is achieved through uninterrupted exchanges and continuous "catastrophes." In addition, starting from the first signs of Judeo-Christian angelology, Angels appear as guardians of time and therefore as the drivers of the course of months and seasons, of the alternation of day and night, of the growth of fruits. Under no circumstances could their meaning ever be given univocally: just like the combinations of the zodiacal signs, their meaning will at different times turn out propitious or impropitious, clear or uncertain. The sign of the Angel is equally protean: now, for this combination of stars, it gleams like the cherub of Pseudo-Dionysius; now, for this other combination, it falls into the animal features of the guardian-idol of Babylon.

But the Babylonian zodiac informs other essential elements in the structure of the angelical Caelum Caeli. In Babylonian mythology the zodiac is understood to be the embankment of Heaven.[14] Its path, along which the seven stars move in seven orbits and seven levels, separates the lower waters from the higher ones, preventing new floods. That is why the rainbow is the image of the zodiac: it is set in memory of the victory over chaos, of the formation of the embankment that runs on high to protect the fertile soil. The signs of the zodiac are the guardian Angels of the embankment, just like the stars are the lords that rule over it and dwell in it. These stars represent the highest manifestation of the divine; they herald and announce the supreme theophany (the star that in ancient times was assigned to the oriental position was called Nebo or Nabu, that is, Nunzio [Messenger], the Greek Hermes). The levels of the zodiac, composed of ever-narrowing circles the higher one rises, lead up to the base of the Throne. The four figures of Cherubim, in short, seem to symbolize the maximum height of the zodiac, that is, its supreme regents. The Babylonian computation of the year began from the Bull; the winged solar disk, the Eagle, symbolized the first manifestation of the divine; under the sign of the Lion, the Eagle-Sun reached its apogee.[15]

The angelical dimension of being seems to constitute itself, ab origine (from the beginning), in the rhythm of this astral necessity. This rhythm still resonates in the Areopagitic macro-mirror, in the correspondences between angelical hierarchies and celestial bodies, and in those between the pure spirits of the Caelum Caeli and the ecclesiastical hierarchies. "The moving heavens, nine in all, speak of the numbers, orders and hierarchies; the tenth proclaims the very unity and stability of God" (Dante, Convivio, II, V, 12; English translation, C. Ryan, trans., The Banquet, Stanford French and Italian Studies series, [ANMA Libri, 1989].) The music of the spheres reproduces the Number of the music of angelical choirs; and its relations (its Logos) inform whatever happens in the mundus sitalis. How can we break the "religio" that attracts this vision of the angelical powers and their spiritual "modesty" to the numerus of the astral procession and of the zodiacal succession? How can we free the Angel from the astrological necessity of this rhythm that incessantly seems to seduce it toward the figures of the idol and demon, contaminating its theophanic function? How can we imagine the "freedom" of the Angel, if its figure is derived from those mythological and zodiacal representations, and still relies on them? Here bursts forth *the* problem of Judeo-Christian angelology. If we want to understand the always ambivalent attitude of Christian theology toward the Angel we have to refer to this problem, and not only to the question—emphasized on numerous occasions by Corbin—of the structural incompatibility between the full recognition of the angelical dimension of being (of the necessity of the Angel) and the dogma of incarnation and trinitarian theology.

This explains the tension, already present in Pseudo-Dionysius, between the representation of the sacred order and the justification of the free will of the angelic creature. Up to the Renaissance, the astrological dispute will develop and accompany all of the twists and turns occasioned by this tension. It is necessary that the immutable nature of the cosmic taxis should not make vain the freedom of the creature. A perfect hierarchy can emerge only from participation, moreover: from the creature's assimilation of that order, from the creature's free attending to it, from its transfiguration into a note of the concentus (symphony) that has in the "unitade et stabilitade" (unity and stability) of God its own Archimusicus (chief musician).[16] But within this concentus, as soon as it is intoned, are Angels not transformed into mere *leitourgika pneumata* (ministering spirits) (Hebrews 1:14), into spirits *destined to serve*?[17] And that critical moment par excellence of the rebellion of the first Angel, does it not finally assume the character of a decision made once and for all? The heavenly angelical zodiac, in fact, forms an embankment against the chaos of Satan's reign; it defends the dwelling place of homo sanus (sound, safe man) in accordance with the "mirabil conseguenza" (marvelous consequence) of its circular deployment. But in fixing—one could say, in petrifying—the decision of Satan, the Angel also fixes itself onto this circuit. "The graduated structure of the world as a concentrical order around God: from the supreme nearness . . . to the extreme 'echo' of divine Names"[18] remains formally identical to that of the astral movement along the zodiac, from the ring of Saturn to that of the moon (as was the case in Babylonian astronomy). How can we separate the aesthetical-imaginative vis of the Areopagite's (and later of Dante's) vision from such an originary mythological "construct"? The "full and established will" (*Paradiso*, XXIX, 63) rivets the Angel to the "ubi," to "that point" on which "the heavens and all nature are dependent" (ibid., XXVIII, 41–42), to that Lord who radiated "into its being" pure act and pure potentiality, while "in the middle such a bond tied up potentiality with act that it is never unbound" (ibid., XXIX, 35–36).[19] Dante renders the light of this knot, of this unbreakable "pact," by the symbol of laughter (a joyful and complete adherence to the loved object) and by the continuous transfiguration of the natural image into sound and color. But as soon as he has to show the obedience of the Angel, its service, and through this service manifest the Angel's beauty, images that belong to the "mythical" necessity of the astral logos, to the "animal" nature of the hayoth, make their return. The Angel appears joyful, but like a *bee* in a garden which never withers. The angelic Host that "as it flies, sees and sings His glory who enamors it and the goodness which made it so great—like a swarm of bees which one moment enflower themselves and the next return to where their work acquires savor—was descending into the great flower which is adorned with so many petals, and thence reascending to where its love abides forever" (ibid., XXXI, 4–12). How could this bee still *decide itself* from that "light in form of a river" that runs "between two banks painted with marvellous spring" (ibid., XXX, 61–63) or from that "secure and joyful kingdom" (ibid., XXXI, 25) on whose mirror is eternally reflected its own laughing beauty? It seems that the only place where the Angel can decide itself remains the originary one that opens the adventure of the whole universe: whence the pole of absolute Evil voluntarily opposes itself to service and praise. All Angels are created in grace, but grace does not violate free will: the devil does not sin when it is created (the Agent does not participate in its sin), but only when it decides to sin (St. Augustine, *De civitate Dei*, XI, 15). The moment of choice, which God deems inalienable, takes over from the general motion toward the Good, proper to every creature: as if He could only reign over a civitas of free wills. A terrible crossroad appears then on the Angel's path, which it must confront; it cannot persist in the natural motion of love for its Maker; the merits of its love will be counted "in termino viae et ultime" ("at the end of the road and lastly").[20] *Here* it must *decide* to love in order to love *totaliter* (completely) at the end. Its love is merely transient until it has pronounced this full Yes. But the possibility of the Yes implies that of negation; that is, the affirmation of a love that is not directed to its own Principle.

Contrary to what happens with man, the Angel could never sin by mistake or out of ignorance or distraction. At the moment of its creation, it is luminously inclined to the Good and to love, both to a love for its Author and for itself. Mirroring itself, the Angel-Narcissus intellectualis can see only its own image as the name of its Principle. But at that crossroads, in that decisive instant, where it is called upon, it is also free to choose and love itself independent of God. On one side stand the Angels that rise up to the vision of their author totaliter; on the other side stand those that remain blinded by their own light. The former turn toward Morning; the latter, *"in seipsis remanentes"* ("remaining in themselves"), swell with pride and are transformed into Night (St. Thomas Aquinas, *Summa theologiae*, Ia, q.63, a.6, ad 4). The light of the creature seduces them from that of the Agent. This occurs not because that light is something evil (it is good, like all created things), but because they love it *inordinately* (in other words, they are not "modest" in their affection), they deny any dependency on its part and affirm its autonomy. "Allecti a pulchritudine suae naturae" ("Powerfully attracted by the beauty of their nature") (St. Thomas Aquinas, *De malo*, q.16, a.12, ad 13), these Angels aspire to be like God, they presume to deify themselves with their own forces, they refuse to participate in the design of grace. In *De malo* (q.16, a.3) Thomas Aquinas adds: "the first sin of the devil consists in wanting supernatural blessedness, which consists in the full vision of God, without having recourse to God." Therefore the Angel falls not because it refuses the beatific vision, but because it refuses to receive it ex misericordia (out of mercy).

The Angel's sin inaugurates that of man in its most proper essence. To "remain in oneself" expresses the nature of sin as *absolute isolator* (as Kierkegaard defined it),[21] as *desperatio* (despair) in regard to every relationship to the Other. Florenskii defined sin as "inhospitable self-affirmation":[22] to love one's own creaturely light so absolutely as to be incapable of offering it, to be incapable of receiving in it any Presupposition. Here comes to a close the circle that began with the theme of the Angel's seduction by man: the beauty (closed inside itself) of man seduced the

Angel—but the Angel itself inaugurated that inhospitable beauty. The Angel was seduced by its own beauty before being seduced by that of the daughters of men. This is the dark side of that same game of mirrors that governs the relation between angelical and terrestrial world. By their sin, Angels reveal the terrible power of free will, its possibility of deciding itself from the Creator Himself,[23] from the Principle that continuously engenders. Sin appears diabolical because it ab-solves not from a determined point or moment, from a chronologically definable beginning, but from the perennial source of creation. Those Angels that chose this way, were they already seduced by man or is it the decision of Angels that men reflect in the kind of sinning admixed with ignorance, unconsciousness, and error, of which they alone are capable?

There is another crisis, though, that appears decisive and irreversible, after which the destinies of Angel and man become entangled. The fallen Angel and man both can *know* that they love themselves absolutely; the Angel will know it perfectly, man will perceive it only in a confused way. In its sin the Angel chooses the archetype of the perfectly enlightened decision; the decisions of man, instead, remain uncertain and compromising, they avoid the irreparable either-or that the Angel confronts with Satanic hubris. Orthodox Catholic angelology insists, nearly univocally, on the irreversibility of the angelic decision. The Angel could not reform itself for it has seen everything with perfect clarity. "For man the time of decisions lasts until death, for the Angel but one instant."[24] Able to create only intelligent wills, God also had to create the Angel as a potential sinner. But the Angel is likewise created in one stroke, perfectly compos sui (self-possessed), in unison with the very instant of the fiat lux. Just as its nature does not evolve or become, so too its knowledge is spared the tiresome itinerary of human knowledge. God grants time to man, whose nature is in becoming, so that he may re-view his choices, but constrains the Angel to one, irreversible either-or. After that instant the figure of the Angel seems to be decided for eternity: decided is the action that the fallen Angel or demon will have to carry out until the Last Judgment; decided is the orbit of the "blissful" Angels, of the heavenly Choir. Decided is the infernal "noise"; decided is the heavenly polyphony. Man is granted becoming (to transform himself, repent, change his mind); the Angel is granted only one instant in

which strikes inexorably a decision that will not admit of repara-
tion, consolation or repentance. In vain man always longs for this
perfect decision, which is the Angel's *damnation*.

The time of the New Angel is thus only one of the possible figures, one of the possible masks, that the time of the Angel, as
instant-time, puts on. *All* Angels originate from that instant, from
the transparent clarity of that instant, in which the power of their
free will, the penalty of being free, is given in an immense, cosmic
blaze. But in this blaze that power also gives out, is consumed.
"The fall is to the angels just what death is to man. There is no time
to repent" (St. John of Damascus, *De fide ortodoxa*, II, 4 (English
translation, *The Orthodox Faith* in *St. John of Damascus, Writings*
[Washington, D.C.: Catholic University of America Press, 1958]),
nor is there time to sin. Man disposes of a whole life to vary sin and
repentance; the freedom of the Angel, instead, is absolutely merci-
less: it knows only one word, it lasts only one instant. For sure, the
light of this angelical decision displays an unattainable greatness
in the eyes of man; it *stands* like the most perfect knowledge,
almost the archetype of the word identical to the thing. Terrible
beauty of the Angel: not only is its choice irreversible, but, when it
falls, it does not condescend to ask for forgiveness. But just here
the circle of our reflections comes to a close: if the Angel's decision
is so inexorable that it will not admit, once *fallen*, of any change,
how is it possible to disentangle its figure from that mythical
necessity betrayed by its own origins? The effort of Scholastic theology to liberate the Angel from every idolatrous contamination is
certainly magnificent; it appears to us as an extraordinary re-
invention of a myth of origin, of the moment that opens the adventure of the universe. To define the Angel as a perfectly spiritual
nature, one could not resolve it totaliter in the act of its creation,
one had to imagine it truly free and so lead it to the fatal crossroads. But now the will of the Angel appears "flexible" only *before*
this instant; the movement of its will turns out to have been perfectly necessitated. After that instant, the figure of the Angel no
longer can vary; Angels are no longer able to "turn" themselves
round and be "treptoi" (persons liable to be turned or changed; the
definition belongs to St. John of Damascus) unlike all the other
creatures that continue to be so. And to the impossibility of ever

repenting there corresponds symmetrically, in Heaven, the impossibility of ever being seduced.

The Angel's course becomes as firm and certain as that of the Platonic soul after it has chosen its daimon, as the course of the stars, as infallible as the embankment formed by the zodiac around the inhabited earth. The human pilgrim, restless Proteus,[25] would then waver between *two necessities*: that of the firm vision of the heavenly Angel ("These substances, since first they were gladdened by the face of God, have never turned their eyes from It, wherefrom nothing is concealed," *Paradiso*, XXIX, 76–78) and that of the infernal zodiac, of the Archons of matter, in their constant calling to the inhospitable despair of sin. We can try to explain why God has set this test for the Angel; we can find an answer to the nature of the Angel's sin. The sympathy between Angel and man is strongest here: analogous is the test that we are subjected to, analogous also is the nature of sin. But this bond seems to break for good once the angelical decision is made, and "a part of the Angels" falls to perturb "the substrate" of the terrestrial world, and the other *remains* (ibid., XXIX, 50–52). At this point, the figure of the Angel concentrates again into an unchanging principle—and the science of this figure is forced to approximate dramatically that astrology from whose coils it desperately had tried to free itself, like the shepherd in Nietzsche's *Zarathustra* had tried to free himself from the Ouroboros of the eternal return of the same.

The Angel is riveted by *its* decision to an ontological state and the "work" it has to accomplish there. Its will is no longer distinguished from the design that emanates from "that point"; it is secure in the vision of the "Triple Light." The Angel's participation and adherence to the "general form of Paradise" (*Paradiso*, XXXI, 52) appear totaliter et ultime (completely and finally): nothing could still revoke them into doubt.[26] There is an abyssal difference with what strikes the "human family," seduced by "blind cupidity," made to resemble "the little child who dies of hunger and drives away his nurse" (ibid., XXX, 139–141). This contrast torments all of Dante's ascent, right up to the last words of Beatrice. But then would the Angel's decision not appear to be its decision *from* man, a choice it makes to negate every choice, a decision *from* all human venture? Not only are the two possible poles of the universe (absolute Evil and perfect Love) separated in that instant, but also (and this is the most profound and disturbing aspect of that moment) the time of human decisions, a time that becomes, a time of transformations and metamorphoses, is separated from the eternal present of *all* the Angels. As if man and Angel were to accompany each other in the "discovery" of sin, only to assume thereafter incommunicable temporal dimensions, separately waiting for the Last Day, when the game will be up also for man, the fever of free will finally cured. The figure of the Angel anticipates for us this extreme event that will restore all the dissensions of freedom and being-at-risk. The necessity that already dominates the Angel will then reaffirm its law over man, who seemed capable of eluding it.

5

APOKATASTASIS

The struggle against the demon would finally end with a great setback. The freedom of the Angel is already decided—and this irrevocable *iam* (already) prefigures perfectly the destiny of man. The pagan cosmos seems to make its return not simply through the power of its images, but for an essential reason: once the great originary *krisis* is overcome, the angelological vision of being also finds its order determined by an inviolable Law. But then what are we to make of the New Angel "confused" with us to the point of forgetting the *order* received up there, of which it had been informed? What are we to make of the narrow door, *always open*, that its figure re-vealed? What to make of the eschaton safeguarded in the idea of representation? What eschatology, in general, can representation still reflect, if the final time is completely prefigured in the origin, in the originary decision, if the dimension of the nondum (not yet) is only chronological and not qualitative, that is, if it does not withhold a novitas with respect to that which resonates in the *iam*, if iam and nondum are bound by a *sive* (or) and not by the venture, the opening, the suspension of the *et* (and)?

Can this idea of an inflexible cosmic taxis, similitudo divinae voluntatis (similar to the divine will), which angelology manifests, "be quite so easily adopted by a Christian theodicy burdened not only with the problem of suffering in general, but also with the specific problem of eternal Hell"?[1] The Inferno of Dante constitutes the unsurpassable image of the irreversibility of the fall. A supreme Justice has judged it for ever. "The laws of the abyss," of the "deep night that ever makes the infernal valley black" (*Purgatorio*,I, 44–46), do not admit of exceptions. It is true that the sinner him-

67

self confesses his own guilt and yearns for the corresponding punishment (in accordance with the terrible juridical objectivism of
retaliation), it is true that in the sinner "fear turns into desire"
(*Inferno*, III, 126), but this occurs under the goad of divine Justice,
of which there remains only the punitive form—the form of
unyielding Right. The souls that Charon the demon gathers and
beats with his oar really do seem characters or spirits controlled by
the demon. The natural simile assumes a metaphysical pregnancy:
"As in autumn the leaves drop off . . . so the wicked seed of Adam"
(ibid., III, 112–117). Justice, precisely the supreme Justice, is manifest here in its most horrible aspect, as *revenge*, "orribil arte" (horrible art). It forces Dante to struggle against any feeling of pity; in
this struggle his teacher is Virgil, the *pagan*: in his eyes, those who
exceed the measure of virtue, of temperantia (moderation), are
only savage beasts. What for Virgil is habitus (natural disposition)
becomes for Dante a difficult acquisition. He lapses continually
into moments of compassion and *communication* with the sinners. But these moments never turn into a radical questioning of
the their state: this state is perfectly accomplished and calling it
into question would amount to a "secret revolt against the wisdom
of God."[2] In the Inferno all hope is banished, suffering is *eternal*,
the souls that inhabit it are *lost*. Like the heavens and the Angels,
hell *endures eternally*.[3] The "miraculous" communications
between these worlds serve only to underscore their absolute separation or to manifest still more harshly the unappealable sentence
that was cast upon the fallen spirits. Virgil can leave the Inferno,
but only because he has traversed it without cowardice or pity
("here must all cowardice be ended"); Beatrice can leave "her ves-
tiges" in the afflicted city, with the lost souls "without hope," but
only because she intends to communicate with Dante (who is still
suspended in life, who is still not judged); the Angel that irrupts
impetuously before the doors of Dis (city of Pluto) to drive away the
"hellish, blood-stained Furies" does not really struggle against the
demonic principle, but merely returns it to its proper place so as to
free the way for Dante. The Fury is not negated but re-placed
within the "orribil arte" of divine Justice. Moreover, in the presence
of the ancient demon, this divine Justice is called by the name of
Fate: "What profits it to butt against the fates?" (*Inferno*, IX, 97); as
if the obsessive tragic wisdom that nothing is stronger than

Anangkē could apply to it, as if it could "translate" pagan Necessity. "And the wretched memorial of Christ's progress through the interior of Hell is a geographic image: a landslide."[4]

In this sense, Dante's most terrible words concern the relation he establishes between this judgment and the Last Judgment. The infernal damnation, then, does not appear as a parenthesis, albeit one full of pain and horribly admixed with the face of Erinyes. Dante did not just see the misery and punishment with which the damned must reintegrate the cosmic order that they have shattered when they lost "the good of the intellect" (measure, modesty, number—as Virgil teaches); he sees the Inferno sub species aeternitatis—he sees, so to speak, *after* the Last Judgment—he sees the cosmic order that will reign *after* this world and this heaven. His "science" admits of no doubts in this regard: here and now it is perfectly possible to answer the question: "Master, will these torments increase after the great judgment, or become less or continue as fierce as now?" (ibid., VI, 103–105). The more perfect a thing is, the more perfect will it be inclined to good (if Goodness is its telos) or to evil. "After the great judgment", the torments of the condemned will be *perfect* (even if only relatively perfect, since the perfect state of a soul is that for which it was created, that is, happiness in the possession of truth and justice). At last united with the body, they will suffer perfectly, just like the blessed will rejoice perfectly (*Inferno*, VI, 103–111). Nothing will have changed in the infernal economy when the souls, reunited with their bodies, return there from the valley of Iehoshaphat: the final Judgment will seal their tombs and confirm the sentence by placing a gravestone (ibid., X, 10–12). For now, "like those with faulty vision," the damned can still see things at a distance; God grants them some sort of prophetic gift. But with the end of the world even this knowledge will have to cease. The sinner will then be *all dead*, completely ignorant and blind (ibid., X, 100–108). The eschatological perspective confirms without pity what was written on the door of the Inferno. But one should rather say that the infernal dimension has swallowed every eschatological tension, has completely removed the words of St. Paul: "Itaque nolite ante tempus quidquam iudicare, quoadusque veniat Dominus, qui et illuminabit abscundita tenebrarum et manifestabit consilia cordium; et tunc laus erit unicuique a Deo" ("Therefore do not pronounce judgment before the time, before the Lord comes, who will bring to light the things now hidden in darkness and will disclose the purposes of the heart. Then every man will receive his commendation from God") (1 Corinthians 4:5).

Dante's Inferno is truly a test bench, not just of the fallen Angel and its victims, but of the whole Christian angelological dimension. If the originary decision is unappealable, if the judgment pronounced after death can be made *perfect* only after "ta prota" ("the first things") have passed away (Revelation 21:1–4; 2 Peter 10), if the Judgment does not "review" but essentially repeats the sentence and the absolute division between the heavenly rose and Hell (a veritable Hades, complete absence of light and vision), then Necessity is the last word in this theology, where the most perfect torment is associated with the most perfect blessedness. The eschatological dimension is, literally, its apocalypse, its final and complete manifestation. We will then see what we can already perfectly know; this "science" is made possible by the fact that the eschaton is also a dimension of Necessity, nothing other than its supreme moment. A "golden chain" links the Justice of revenge and retaliation, so juridically and rationally formalized, to the Last Judgment, even though the latter participates in the mystery of the Parousia. His return can essentially change nothing; He comes to complete and to perfect, not to redeem or to promise redemption. He comes to judge anew, as if the first time He had also come for this purpose. A Christ who "surrenders forever to the Father's cosmic will"[5] condemns judged men along with *all* Angels to the yoke of Necessity. This is why it is so important that the fallen Angel be represented as a rigid demon, petrified in its dimension, just like, at "the apex of the rose," the heavenly Angels are to perform their circles like signs of a happy zodiac, like stars, like bees.

From the beginning, other currents of the tradition have reacted against the literally catastrophic consequences of this vision for the essence of Christian faith, a vision which is that of Scholastic orthodoxy, from Augustine to Thomas Aquinas. The conflict at issue, for sure, unfolds within the general framework of this tradition. Both in the Old and New Covenants the punishment is explicitly defined as eternal, eternal is the fire of hell. But this idea must appear intrinsically antinomical to the set of themes that inform the apocalyptic *transensus* (transition) as soon as it is viewed in light of the very principle of creation ("the goodness of the created being") and, more specifically, of the symbol of Christ. If the transensus resolved itself in Judgment and Sentence it would not be a transensus at all, but something completely deducible from the facts and the evolution of this Age; this is what occurs in Dante. Apocalypse would not mean the regeneration of the events in the world, but rather their perfect rationalization-systematization—a rationalization of which we already possess the key, if only we use correctly the good of the intellect. The apocalyptic transensus is reduced to the final instance of a perfectly rationalized juridical-penal procedure. But how could this vision be reconciled with the originary and never disavowed "goodness" of creation? Is this "goodness" not reaffirmed, beyond all of its crises, in the mystery of the resurrection? And is this mystery not central to the symbol of Christ? If God has sent his Son into the world it cannot be for the sake of announcing a Judgment; there is no need for the sacrifice of the Son in order to judge. He has been sent "ut salvetur mundus per ipsum" ("that the world might be saved through him") (John 3:17).[6] This annunciation must concern the entire cosmos, for as a whole it yearns to reintegrate the originary "goodness" that was lost in the fall, but which was not completely destroyed with it. If the eschaton cruelly confirmed the division, proper to this world, of Light and Darkness, indeed if it absolutized the division, this would necessarily imply the *failure* of the Son. The Logos of the Son would not have succeeded in ex-pressing anew the creature *to* the Father; the Logos would have remained mute, it would not have spoken to the Father—it would not have succeeded in making its existence a perfect *exegesis-to-the-Father* of the creature. Forever *unexpressed* with regard to the Father, *alone* in front of Him, the creature would remain separated from Him by the abyss thrown open by the fall. Nothing less than the meaning of the New Covenant is at stake in the vision of the apocalypse as the time of the supreme judgment, that is: of the supreme division.

> But communion with God is life and light, and the enjoyment of all the benefits which He has in store. But on as many as, according to their choice, depart from God, He inflicts that separation from Himself which they have chosen of their own accord. . . . Inasmuch, then, as in this world some persons betake themselves

to the light, and by faith unite themselves with God, but others shun the light, and separate themselves from God, the Word of God comes preparing a fit habitation for both. For those indeed who are in the light, that they may derive enjoyment from it, and from the good things contained in it; but for those in darkness, that they may partake in its calamities. (St. Irenaeus, *Against Heresies*, V, 27–28; English translation, *The Ante-Nicene Fathers*, vol. 1, p. 556 Grand Rapids, Mich.: W. Eerdmans, 1985).

But if the triumph of the Son in the Parousia is understood instead as *the* redemption of creation, there result no less paradoxical, "scandalous" consequences. The first, and least disquieting, regards the fact that the figure of the Son remains *incomplete* even after the resurrection and the ascension. The true end of the kenosis is given only in the dimension of the eschaton. The Taboric Light is nothing other than the prefiguration and anticipation of the Parousia, the eucharistic sacrifice is likewise the promise of the Parousia. The incompleteness of the world mirrors that of the Heavens. In the Heavens Christ *awaits* his own definitive resurrection, which will be such only in the resurrection of the creature.[7] His passion, says Pascal, lasts until the advent of that day. This vision overturns the hierarchical order perfectly resolved in the Heavens of Dante. In the second place, it is inevitable to think the Parousia as being addressed to *all* creatures, for each entity of the world cannot be understood as a note of the same cosmos until the last Foe (and Foe precisely of this being-cosmos of the world) is vanquished. The resurrection reintegrates the originary eternity of the created being,[8] putting an end to its "image"; that is, to what in the world comes from the world and not from the Father (1 John 2:15–17). But the resurrection as regeneration of the world (reintegration of its own nature as eternal cosmos) transforms the place and function of *all* entities. Nothing is as before. The transensus cannot concern only human beings, for their regeneration would also transfigure the totality of correspondences and relations. Therefore all beings endowed with logos await the Logos; He has come and will come again in the interest of all. *Also for the stars*, because in the eyes of God "even the stars are not completely pure" (Origen, *Commentarium in Joannem*, I, 35). The benefits of Christ's sacrifice extend from the creatures of the earth to those of the heavens. Origen, whom Meister Eckhart called "the great

Teacher,"[9] adumbrates the idea of a double sacrifice: for human beings, Christ shed "the very bodily matter of his blood, whilst for the celestial creatures . . . he offered the vital strength of his body as some kind of spiritual sacrifice" (*Homilies on Leviticus*, I, 3; English translation, G. W. Barkley, *The Fathers of the Church*, vol. 83 [Washington, D.C.: Catholic University of America Press, 1991]). The passion of Christ takes place also in Heaven.[10]

These disconcerting ideas are imposed on us by the need to understand the grace of the Second Coming beyond every "chronological" tie to the actual world, in the fullness of its redemptive word and in harmony with the radical meaning of the Annunciation itself: the Sacrifice inaugurates an epoch that no longer obeys the Nomos, that is no longer the servant of Nomos, but is the epoch of *Charis and Alētheia* (Grace and Truth). The Nomos judges no longer; it is no longer left up to the Nomos to judge on the basis of works. If this were the case, Christ would have died in vain. The vision of the apocalypse that is fixated on the dimension of Judgment is essentially nomothetic. Instead, it is not the triumph of the Nomos, but the unveiling of the power of Grace that constitutes its promise. But this promise must be thought as addressed to *all*, and therefore also to iniquitous spirits. Not only human beings, heavenly Angels, and stars (whose image, as we know, is related to the Angel), but also the demon itself, the fallen Angel itself, will be transfigured in the Parousia, for it seems untenable that the eschaton will not re-create the originary unity, will not abolish the inhospitable separation of sin. The cosmic *krisis* that sin continuously reproduces cannot be negated by a new *sanction*, but by an act of Charis, by a supreme Gift that *opens* every isolation, every separation, every autonomy (and therefore opens the foundation itself of every autonomy, which is Nomos), that *opens* a new Age in which ripens the redemption of all heavenly, earthly and infernal creatures, and this redemption can ripen because they finally participate in it. If this *transensus* is not conceivable, not only does the *fire* of the New Covenant, which affirms the epoch of Charis and Alētheia, in contrast to that of Nomos, remain without nutriment; not only does the mystery of resurrection, far from figuring a new image of the entire creation, resolve itself into the perfection of its current state (as in Dante); but it is the whole design of redemption that fails, for a part of creation (and it is of no import to know which one or how much) does not participate in it.

None of the entities of creation "ab illa etiam finali unitate ac convenientia discrepabit" ("is to differ wholly from the final unity and fitness of things"). All orders of creation—even those that "sub principatu diaboli agunt ac malitiae eius obtemperant" ("act under the government of the devil and obey his wicked commands")—will be provided for "pro ordine, pro ratione" ("in accordance to their order and nature"). Even they "aliquando in futuris saeculis converti ad bonitatem" ("will in a future world be converted to righteousness"). Indeed, they cannot have absolutely lost their liberi facultas arbitrii (faculty of free will), which is the terrible gift granted to rational creatures. "In this way, first some and then others," after painful penalties and severe corrections, will be reintegrated "first among the angels and then even among the Virtues of the higher stages." They will be able to reach, one stage at a time, from one officium (function) to the other, "usque ad ea quae sunt invisibilia et aeterna" ("to those [realities] that are invisible and eternal"), in virtue of Grace and free will, the latter finally entering into synergy with the former. Only then will the habitus of this world—understood in a radical sense—come to an end (Origen, *De Principiis*, I, 6, 3). This Origenian idea[11] (which should not be defined as a "philosophical optimism" because it corresponds thoroughly to the problematic of the Annunciation) was recovered by St. Gregory of Nyssa. The Parousia initiates, is the *source* of, "a univocal song of thanksgiving from the whole of creation." This song is also the return to the originary condition of "those who are now lying in Sin" (sub principatu diaboli) (*The Great Catechism*, XXVI, 8 English translation in *Nicene and Post-Nicene Fathers*, vol. V. [Grand Rapids, Mich.: Eerdmans, 1954]). One day there will have to be established "an accord in Goodness" between all rational creatures, angels, human beings and subterranean spirits, that today find themselves in separate states of being. After an exceedingly long period of time, "there will remain nothing but Goodness" (*On the Soul and the Resurrection*). The *apokatastasis* equally implies for St. Gregory of Nyssa the noneternal character of hell, the redemption of the devil, which originates in the apocalyptic transensus. The apocalyptic event—the most *individual* imaginable (en atomōi), similar to the briefest blink of the eye—promises the final apokatastasis. For this reason, it is not the End, but *source* of a new Heaven and a new Earth.[12]

This idea of Parousia and the redemptive function of the apocalyptic event is destined to cast a disconcerting light on the first Coming. It, too, appears as the supreme Gift, absolutely *gratuitous*. There is no determinate reason for it; it is not animated by a human, all too human purposive scheme. The first Coming is a prefiguration of the sovereign Charis of the apokatastasis. "The death of our Lord was not to save us from our sins, not at all, it was for no other purpose than to show to the world the charity of God for his creation." The incarnation and sacrifice of God would not have been necessary to grant the forgiveness of sins.[13] "The coming of Christ to the world and His death is completely diminished if we make it the cause of our redemption from sin. . . . Why then do we blame sin, if it has provided us with all these goods?" Is sin so strong as to require of God such a sacrifice? And is our idea of God so miserable as to imprison it in this purposive scheme? God went so far as to suffer insults and spits, to give his Son solely to show His Grace, gratuitously, for love, just as for love He was moved to creation.[14] Only the "sublime charity of the creator" *gives itself* in the creation and in the Passion, a charity that *offers itself*, exceeding every determinate end (perhaps even that of the forgiveness of sins). Saint Isaac of Nineveh (whom we have been quoting from the gnostic *IV Centuria*) explicitly affirms the orthodox character of such conceptions, through citations of Theodore of Mopsuestia and Diodore of Tarsus—conceptions that constitute the basis of the teachings on Gehenna of the Elder Zosima that conclude the second part of *The Brothers Karamazov*.[15]

It is not only Angels that will overcome this fear and trembling that has entered and lives in their own Heavens ever since they saw one of them fall ("they despaired of themselves because they believed that they would all fall," Isaac of Nineveh, *IV Centuria*, 80), a suffering that, after the first Coming, they "joyously" accepted, encouraged by the hope of things to come, but that cannot be said to have as yet completely vanished. Not only will all men form one Church, finally convinced by the direct vision of Truth that offers itself to us out of grace—but demons themselves *at last* "will be made perfect, out of the grace of their creator" (Isaac of Nineveh). Isaac calls them "a precious stone slipped

into the abyss." It is evil to think "that the sinners in Hell are desti-
tute of love for the Creator" (Isaac of Nineveh, *Mystic Treatises*,
XXVII; English translation, A. J. Wensinck, *Mystic Treatises by
Isaac of Nineveh* [Amsterdam, 1923], p. 136), but it is still a sign of
a lack of compassion and love to think that those who were created
good out of grace (and Angels, according to certain traditions, were
created even before the fiat lux, in the Silence that precedes the
Word) may never reintegrate their own origin. This would mean
setting a radical limit to the power of Grace, subjecting it to the
Nomos and the judgment on works that the Nomos pronounces: a
juridical vision of Grace, founded on the respect of a sort of *unalterable* Grundnorm (fundamental norm). If death (or the originary
fall) poses a limit to the possibility of mercy and expiation, then
God is subject to death. This is why the completion of creation is
not its judgment but its redemption, understood as the truth-
unveiledness of the proper nature of each entity: "the will of God is
to universalize everything, to elevate everything into a unity with
light." In this work of universalization and elevation God Himself
becomes, is life, has a destiny, subjects Himself to suffering, suffers
from the antithesis: "without the concept of a God who suffers in a
human way . . . the whole of history remains incomprehensible."[16]
Fall and death and sacrifice and apocalypse—all of this is necessary
to fulfill the purpose of creation: that goodness be elevated from
Darkness into actuality, so as to live in God everlastingly.[17] The
fourth Gospel, which announces-promises the Apocalypse, coincides with the unveiling of the perfect Grace that is capable of ele-
vating the dia-bolic principle itself into unity with the Light.

    Moreover, did not this principle affirm itself as a jealous and
intransigent love? And, as love, did it not have to suffer throughout
the whole expanse of time the most painful nostalgia for the loss of
its Object? In his *Mathnawi*, Rumi expounds grandiosely this idea:

> Satan answered: . . . How can the first love come out of the heart?
> Even if you were to travel from Rum to Khotan, how can the love
> of your native land be wrenched out of your soul? I was also
> drunk of this wine once, I was also one of those lovers in the
> court of God! . . . Who was it that went looking for my milk when
> I was a child? Who used to rock my cradle? . . . And if the sea of
> generosity has now rebuked me, how can those doors of grace
> remain eternally closed? He has created the world as an act of

love, His sun caresses even the smallest atoms of dust. And the separation, full of His wrath, is surely nothing but a means to get to know better the value of the union with Him. And now, in these few days in which He keeps me away, my eyes remain always fixed on His sublime face! . . . And even in this suffering I savor His presence: by Him I have been defeated, defeated, defeated!

How can one think such a paradox? how can one try to say such a "scandal": that the Accuser itself, the supreme Angel whose voluntary fall was designed to *condemn* the creation of man, may in the end participate in the sole Church? Every representation of the eschaton (indeed every representation, if representation as such is endowed with eschatological force) must confront these questions. Around them turns what is perhaps the only great eschatological text of the twentieth century, *L'Epouse de l'agneau* by Sergei Boulgakov.[18]

The Judgment is already contained in the Parousia; every human being judges himself or herself in the face-to-face with the return of Christ. The Last Judgment is interiorized (ibid., pp. 346–348). Man is not judged like a servant is judged by the master, but like a free son he finally comes to recognize the abysmal distance from Truth that had marked his existence. Christ is not the Judge, but each man judges himself in Him and suffers horribly from not having recognized Him earlier. This means that each man, in this eschatological dimension, which is a supreme theological drama, contains in himself inseparably hell, darkness, and love. Who will have no sins to confess face to face with Him? And, in seeing Him, who will not love Him and judge himself for love? *Inside man himself* resonates a judgment that condemns his mortal figure and saves his divine idea. Man will never be more divided and lacerated: one of his parts will join with Glory itself and the other will suffer the punishments of hell. The separation between torment and blessedness must be understood only in this sense: it is inward and relative to each one (ibid., p. 351). Isaac of Nineveh had already said it: "even those who are scourged in Hell are tormented with the scourgings of love. . . . The suffering which takes hold of the heart through the sinning against love is more acute that any other torture" (*Mystical Treatises*, p. 136). That eternal life and damnation and death may be conceived simultaneously is the unsurpassable antinomical postulate of an eschatology capable of a radical adherence to the redemptive, nonaccusatorial function of Christ, to the dimension of his Annunciation that belongs to Charis and Alētheia, not to the Nomos.

The future Age, the new Heaven and the new Earth therefore cannot be conceived as immobile, and even less as being of infinite duration. They constitute the theater of the creative assimilation of God by the creature. To the apex of the perfectly gratuitous manifestation of divine Love (Gift-Charis that it would be "base" to associate with any finite end) there corresponds in man, through the suffering provoked by the recognition of his past deformity with respect to that Image, a free *opening*, a free emptying of the self to receive that Gift, itself a "gesture" that awaits or expects nothing, that questions nothing, that is moved only by the torment of not being perfect Love. Not only is the freedom of the rational creature not destroyed in the face-to-face with the Parousia, but only now does it truly unfold as such. Only those actions that follow the apocalyptic transensus are truly free—because only in the future Age will acting no longer be determined by contingent causes, by physico-natural concatenations and successions. Here and now no one could completely extricate oneself from such interest, no one could completely avoid waiting-questioning-expecting, avoid acting *in the service* of the thing and of the purpose. In the future Age, instead, every servile relation is destroyed; our freedom is no longer *distracted* and can finally attend *gratuitously* to its End. Freedom itself *resurrects*: the resurrected body wants a resurrected freedom. Father and Son reciprocally offer themselves in the Open, in the Alētheia, without the mediation of the "many names," the confusion of the many principles that necessarily dominates this world.

Blessedness and damnation face each other in every man. Any abstract separation of the two dimensions is dia-bolical (Boulgakov, *L'Epouse de l'agneau*, p. 367). Any petrification of Evil that decrees its unredeemability, any judgment that tears apart in an absolute fashion the dimension of Evil from that of Good, any form of rationalistic-moralistic dualism reduces the divine Charis to the function of Nomos. But the gaze of Nomos has no claim to totality because it is constitutively the gaze of judgment-division. Separ-

ating the whole into parts through its sentences, it incessantly re-
creates the same inhospitable self-affirmation that is the quintessence of sin. The "circle" between Nomos and sin, which St. Paul
(Romans 7:7) identifies in words of extraordinary tension, can be
broken only if one conceives of (each one's) hell as a free act of love
for God (ibid, p. 371), as a process that *frees* from hell. The entire
eschatological dimension appears, then, as the creature's address-
ing of the Other, as a giving place in itself to the Other by the creature. This dimension, far from eternalizing difference by fossilizing
it into Paradise and Hell, considers it only as the beginning (in
each creature), as the initial tension toward that receptive offering
of itself of all in all that constitutes the fire of the promise of the
first Coming.[19]

If just one part of creation persists in its being-part, if the dia-
bolical principle can resist even in the most insignificant fragment
of creation, the sense of creation ends in a setback. The eternaliza-
tion of infernal punishments (this pedagogy of fear, this peniten-
tiary psychology, as Boulgakov calls it) only demonstrates the
impotence of spirit, pneuma, and dissolves its work of participa-
tion-communication. But how will Satan itself open up to the
Spirit? How is it conceivable that the principle of separation will
abolish itself, assume into itself an energy which effects its annihilation? In man, as we saw, openness to the Other and inhospitable
self-affirmation coexist dramatically; but how can Satan's diabolical nature not be complete and perfect? The Parousia can convince
man of the Truth, can cure the angelic Choir of the fear and trembling that torments it ever since the fall, but will it be sufficient to
initiate a *metanoia* (repentance) of Satan itself, of the Angel that
has affirmed its own autonomy face to face with God? If one
answers in the negative then divine mercy suffers a radical limita-
tion and is subjected to a Nomos. It becomes one act of the cosmos
among many, a part, unable to subsume in its pneuma the differences in their abstract oppositions. But how can one conceive of an
affirmative answer? Certainly, by virtue of a symmetry with the
originary freedom of sin, nothing seems to prohibit now the fallen
Angel from freely repenting and participating-corresponding to
the action of Grace. It realizes that the freedom that it claimed
from the Principle, its own solipsistic affirmation, is simply void,

reverts into nothing; that is, its activity in the world has manifested itself only in the form of a simple negation of communication and relation, in the form of the absolute *isolator*. But why should it come to this realization now, in the "atom" of the apocalypse? Was its knowledge as weak as that of man so that it stands in need of this instant, of the persuasive power of the Parousia? Does the dia-bolical principle in itself not always already accuse itself? If this principle is absolutely dia-bolical (and we cannot conceive of it otherwise), then it is ab origine negation of itself, self-annihilation. If Satan were to entertain with itself a positive relation of preservation, attention, defense, it would no longer be itself, it would enter in communication with itself. Its self-affirmation is absolutely inhospitable, and thus it is inhospitable with regard to itself. Satan negates itself in its own self-affirmation.

Only in this way, and not as a process that "evolves" starting with the Parousia, does it seem possible to imagine the "exhaustion" of Hell. At issue is a movement internal to Evil that inexorably cancels its very predicability. How could Satan oppose itself to this logic that overdetermines its activity? Either it is a completely autonomous principle, originally just like God, and then nothing, no manifestation or apocalypse will ever suffice to convince it and no metanoia is applicable to it (it would be like applying it to God himself); or it must necessarily negate itself in the end, but the latter option is comprehensible on the basis of an inviolable "logic"—in the quintessence of sin lies the movement that shows its own nothingness. But if this is the case, then one must necessarily conclude that Evil and sin cannot subsist, they have no real subsistence, because that movement, that "logic" on the basis of which they negate themselves, has always already begun, it is their own since the first fall. It makes no sense to affirm that with the Parousia begins the annihilation of Hell, nor, strictly speaking, can one say that Evil is destined to nothing, for Evil is constitutively nothing, nothing but the determination of being that is negated as soon as it is considered, which is impossible to think as something having any form of subsistence whatsoever. To attribute freedom and will to this determination is simply absurd. What separates itself from the whole and "becomes conceited of its beauty", what presumes to fix itself in the separateness of its in-itself, must *of necessity* be negated. This movement, in all of its stages, belongs to the whole. The autonomy of Satan becomes nothing other than a moment of the whole; that is, it is shown to be as such completely illusory. It merely expressed the determination of the whole in its parts—the "intellectualism" of considering the parts as separated from the whole. Lucifer, then, is nothing but the *moment* of "God's wrath towards himself in his alterity."[20]

Even the most radical attempt to bend the inexorability of the Judgment, to overcome the ontological fixity of Angels and demons, seems to conclude itself again under the shadow of necessity—a logical-gnosiological necessity, for in no other form is the self-"emancipation" of Satan conceivable. The eschatological perspective, which from Origen and Gregory of Nyssa surfaces again in Boulgakov, *founders* the vision of the apocalypse as Judgment, the penal-juridical and dualistic conception of Paradise and Hell, the subjection of Charis to Nomos, but seems to collapse under the weight of the problem of the Angel's freedom, where the latter is most terribly in evidence: in the freedom of the fallen Angel.[21] The redemption of this Angel is conceivable only if one eliminates its freedom or, better, shows it to be nothing other than a moment of God's manifestation, always already comprehended in the "economy" of such manifestation. The conclusion appears constitutively antinomical: if the will is essentially free, nothing can obligate Satan to repent (but should one not say this also of man himself? It is true that man would never have imagined the redemptive energy offered by the image of the triumphant Christ, but, if he remains free also in the face of it, why could he not still refuse it?)—if, vice versa, the persistence of the dia-bolical principle condemns all of creation to failure, the overcoming of this principle is conceivable only in terms of its *necessary* self-destructiveness. A destiny inexorably burdens the fallen Angel (and thus the entire genus of Angels), just as it burdened pagan demons. "If you ask me: will there still be eternal punishments? I will answer: yes. But if you ask me: will there be a universal reintegration in blessedness? I will again answer: yes. . . . In the face of the antinomy faith is necessary, given that it is impossible to submit it to reason. It's a yes and a no, and this is the best proof of its religious significance."[22] The conclusion of Florenskii must not be understood in a negative or apophatic sense; the antinomical nature of eschatology is coherent with the antinomical character of the Annunciation itself[23]—of that Truth which comprehends in itself its own Cross, of that Word which right at its climax ceases to speak and turns into a cry. Moreover, that the eschaton should have to be thought antinomically, much more than a sign, perhaps this represents *the* sign of the profoundly ir-religious form of this "religion."[24] The redemption it promises cannot be attained through any method, any univocal and clearly projectable path. Its truth cannot be defined nomothetically; it cannot be reduced to the path of Day in contrast to that of Night. Any attempt to rationalize it—that is, to render it univocal—betrays it. It remains concealed in the pure possible of the gratuitous communicating-participating of all dimensions of being—a harmony that is, like the Platonic Good, beyond every determination of being. On the threshold of this possible, or rather in its Opening, ever present yet never discursively graspable (idea of creation and thus everywhere and nowhere, ou-topia of creation), are ventured the creatures, humans and Angels, in all the multiplicity of the names with which they call forth and push away, listen to and seduce each other.

6

BIRDS
OF THE SOUL

So the Angel is a contestant (agōnistēs),[1] an essential protago-
nist of the drama: it plays suspended between all the axes of creation. It lives in the beginning as well as in the eschaton; it
represents antinomically necessity and freedom, both animal-
zodiac-star and perennial energy of decision. This is why the Angel
stands in the risk of that Opening—if it were only decision, a decision founded on nothing and related to nothing, the Angel would
dwell safely in it. But a decision is always a decision from other, and
it can never be absolute; if it were absolute, it would manifest a
dimension of necessity and so turn into its opposite. Angelical is
that dimension of being in which the determinations, obtaining
separately in the other creatures, articulate themselves by juxtaposition and resonate simultaneously, in which the antinomy of creation manifests itself polyphonically. It is in this light that we have
to reconsider the figures encountered previously.

What appeared to be a simple contradiction can be expressed
as the constitutive antinomy of the characters of the Angel. Such
is the case with its being-animal. The creature that on earth
comes closest to this trait of the Angel, by which it appears
decided in its decision, necessitated by it, is the animal. The Angel
is called *cherub* and *butterfly* and *bee* because of this affinity. The
Angel "emparadizes" (or demonizes) the animal. *Mehr Vogel* . . . is
the title given by Klee to one of his drawings on the theme of the
Angel: more bird . . . than Angel. Birds of the soul is what Rilke
calls them.[2]

Dante's angelology is dominated by this motif (and it could not be otherwise given that precisely in Dante the idea of the Angel, of all Angels, as entities inexorably placed in the cosmic order finds the harshest expression). Since the Angel's knowledge is a direct intuition, since the identity of knowing and seeing (which "prevails" in all of our culture) is perfect in it, anyone who attributes to it the all too human faculty of memory is daydreaming (*Paradiso*, XXIX, 79–82); the visio facialis makes the "art" of memory useless for it. (Notorious is Dante's polemic here with St. Bonaventure's conception, *Breviloquium*, II, 6, 2). Hence the Angels will not even remember the decision that divided them into two reigns. The absence of fear and trembling in Dante's Angel is explained by this perfect forgetfulness. Only man remembers the instant of that decision; only man knows the adventure and the sin of the Angel. But how will the Angel, on its part, know anything of man, if it has no idea of the deepest suffering tormenting his existence: the necessity of remembrance? Rilke's themes concerning the distance of the Angel find here their proper theological foundation. The wave of our Erinnerungsleben (life of remembrance) can, at times, surprise the Angel, but it never participates therein. Dante gets to admire the triumph and living light of the angelical Choir, but no Angel calls him and speaks to him. If the originary decision of the Angel is an irreversible has-been, then it is necessary for it to lose its memory and for its own wait to be represented as the instantaneous reflection of the Light it praises. We are the sole guardians of memory; it is Tobias who moves in search of the message that Raphael has forgotten—it is Mary who dictates the words of the Annunciation to Gabriel. It is not because we want to be "taken to heart" that we invoke the Angel, but on the contrary we do so out of nostalgia for that perfect forgetfulness of which the Angel is master, nostalgia for the complete Lēthē, "satisfied" with itself, that coincides with the same vision at whose source the Angel incessantly nourishes its own light. In Dante, the happiness of the Angel connotes oblivion.

But Beatrice, Madonna of Intelligence, does not only explain why it is a dream to maintain that the Angel possesses memory. On earth, "in your schools," one also errs in affirming that the Angel understands and wills (*Paradiso*, XXIX, 70–72). The work of the "swarm of bees" does not proceed discursively and intentionally.

The "animal" metaphor therefore seems to be something more than a simple metaphor: a truly symbolic bond seems to run between the necessity of angelical "work," riveted to its present and its Light, and the life of the animal, of the creature as animal, between the a-intentional and oblivious simplicity of the Angel and the innocence of the animal. In the *Homilies on Creation*, quoted previously, Narsai captured this profound sympathy between the mute creature that obeys the order of its Author and the Angel that serves-participates in that order from the heights of its incorruptible being. Animal and Angel reflect one another, and in this reflection praise the power of the Creator to which are submitted, in one, both the force of the Angel's direct *intueri* (gaze) and the infinite misery of the animal (*Homélie V*, in *Homélies sur la création*, 141–158). But also the Angel's praise is *silent*. Just as its understanding and willing should not be thought from our discursive and intentional perspective, so too its hymn should not be confused with the time of our earthly music. The time of the Angel's hymn is also *aevum* (this is how Thomas Aquinas, in *De substantiis separatis*, defines the dimension of time in which the Angels dwell). The angelic exultations described by Dante are sparks, fires, gleaming of stars, instantaneous flights—they lack speech, they are not dis-cursive. Symbol, up there, of the most perfect prayer of the heart.[3] But a more adequate symbol would have been the humilitas (humility) of the animal's gaze. It is the she-ass that sees the Angel.

Dante theorizes the Angel as mute creature in *De vulgari eloquentia*, I, 2–3: "for man alone among existing things was given the capacity for speech, since he alone needed it. Neither angels nor lower animals have any need for speech" (English translation, R. S. Haller, *On Eloquence in the Vernacular*. [Lincoln: University of Nebraska Press, 1973], p. 4).[4] To announce their own "glorious thoughts" the Angels have "a most immediate and ineffable capacity of the intellect," by means of which each makes itself completely known to the others. Just as in the inferior animal instinct is one with its nature, so too intelligence and reflection are in the Angel: for the Angel, to know is to reflect in the instant the Light around which it circles eternally. Its intelligence is immediately speculative, just as the behavior of the animal, its habitus, reflects without mediation its most proper nature. The Angel's spiritual speculation proceeds spontaneously from its nature, like "actions and passions" proceed from that of the animal. This is the pure infancy of the Angel—but equally in–fant* is the animal. This correspondence establishes a veritable axis of the cosmic order: on one side, up there, intelligence without memory or language; on the other side, down here, nature without the "seduction" of actions and passions. Both are mute, the Angel and the animal, because both are strangers to the "commercium" that our ratio (reason) institutes, a ratio that "vel circa discretionem vel circa iudicium vel circa electionem diversificatur in singulis" ("on the levels of discernment, or judgment, or will . . . it would seem that almost everyone takes pleasure in being a species to himself") (ibid., p. 5). Precisely at the apex of its speculative force, the figure of the Angel manifests this disconcerting affinity with the other infancy, that of the animal. Their zodiacs are intertwined, and it seems that the same necessity comprehends them.

In the "yellow of the eternal Rose" (*Paradiso*, XXX, 124) flash Angel and bee and butterfly. The form of the rose compresses them indissolubly: a complete form that knows how to remain self-contained in spite of its infinite circles—like the myriads of Angels around their invisible "ubi."

> Rose, O you completely perfect thing
> always self-contained and yet
> spilling yourself forever—O head
> of a torso with too much sweetness missing"
> (Rilke, *The Roses*, III; in *The Complete French Poems of R. M. Rilke*).

In a letter (*Briefwechsel 1914–1921*, [Leipzig, 1938], p. 94), Rilke compares the interior of the rose (the space that "sans cesse / se caresse," as he says in another poem taken from the collection in French dedicated to the Flower) to an angelic dwelling. The Angels are at home in the "great unity"; they inhabit that ou-topic dimension that unites-divides being-there and the Beyond. The rose is the symbol of this dimension; its completeness is like the memory of this "great unity" (but Rilke calls the interior of the rose "völlig bewusst," fully aware).[5]

Rilke's quotation of Dante's image is evident, but so is the profound transformation that this image undergoes. In Dante the Angel's silence maintains a necessary relation to the movements of the terrestrial world; theirs is another time, another nature, but the possibility of communication between us and those separate substances remains assured, as the Poet's journey toward the Eye of the totality demonstrates. This possibility is transformed in Rilke into a pure questioning. Could Angels ever turn to us? And what would they see if they did so?

> The Angel's view: perhaps the tips of trees
> are roots that drink the skies;
> and in the earth the beech's deepest
> roots look like silent summits.
> For them, is not the earth transparent
> against a sky full as a corpse?"
> (*Orchards*, 38; ibid.).

The point of view of the Angels overturns the parameters of our sensible horizon. Their rose, which caresses and contains itself, will it not enclose them so perfectly as to prevent even one of their looks from reaching us? Even if this Angel-Narcissus turned its gaze beyond its rose, our earth, this seemingly solid earth, would seem to it but a transparent wind. Nothing could keep it down here.

Again, the only image, "In the yellow of the rose," that points to us, the only possible passage between the Angel's intelligence without shadows and the fleeting multiplicity of our memories, tongues, expectations appears to be that of the animal. The affinity that presented itself in terms of a mythical Anangkē or in the rhythm of an inviolable astro-logy, now moves, like at the end of an extenuating spiral, in the space of a mute forgetfulness. This animal, which lacks memory, nor understands or wills in the sense that we attribute to these terms, this persecuted and beaten Narcissus is down here the only sign of the incorporeal and incorruptible other one. The animal does not know this, and even if it knew it could not tell—but precisely its in–fancy announces it. This explains the perfect correspondence between Rilke's *Letter to Witold von Hulewicz* and the images of Dante's angelology. Just like Dante's "swarm," "fanning their sides" (*Paradiso*, XXXI, 18), flies from the flower to the beehive, "where its love abides forever" (*Paradiso*, XXXI, 12), so we "butinons éperdument le miel du visible, pour l'accumuler dans la grande ruche d'or de l'Invisible" ("gather the honey of the visible in order to accumulate it in the great golden beehive of the Invisible"). When we stamp "this provisional, perishing earth into ourselves so deeply, so painfully and passionately, that its being may rise again, 'invisibly', in us," our "labor" is essentially analogous to that of Dante's bees. "We are the bees of the Invisible"—but whereas the "operari" (doing) of the bee-Angel insists in the fullness of the Rose, unaware of any venture beyond such perfection (and does not even remember what came before this dwelling), in Rilke the bee has memory, language, intention. It is as though the necessity of Dante's angelology (coherent expression of the general vision of the *Divine Comedy*) had been overwhelmed by that eschatological pneuma that Dante, as we saw in the previous chapter, fixes in the dimension of the *iam*.

We save the thing in the invisible essentially through language, for that symbolical dimension of the name, of which the perfect in–fancy of the Angel knows nothing. To the Angel this redemption would appear a desperate task, and in fact *desperately* "we collect the honey of the visible" (Rilke). But precisely the instant of this despair creates that sudden fracture in the apparently continuous fabric of the visible and of its words, wherein we can recollect (*ri-cor-dare*) "the provisional, perishing earth." In this instant one notices the wings of Gabriel; in this instant begin our astral friendships with the Angel. In Dante, the honey that the Angel collects from the mystical Rose is safe in the golden beehive where it is deposited; no memory and no wait will ever perturb it; no forgotten question will ever put it at risk again. But the same "animal" figure flashing in its light suffices to show how much it partakes of the Jesus patibilis (passible Jesus) that marks the face of every creature—and thus how much it corresponds to the eschatological questioning that is incessantly renewed by this suffering.

It is true that the face of the animal seems to have down here the same direction as that of the Angel; both face the Open, look into "das Offene" (*Eighth Elegy*, 1–2), whereas our eyes are always "reversed." "What *is* outside, we know from the animal's face alone." The constructions of the world reproduced by thought, the "gedeutete Welt," fill human eyes; those of the animal, instead, like deep mirrors of the Open, move "ins Freie";

> the free animal
> has its decease perpetually behind it
> and God in front, and when it moves, it moves

into eternity, like running springs.
(*Eighth Elegy*, 10–13)

With the same *measure*, in Dante, the Angel circles the Point, on which it fixes "face and love." And "the pure space before us, such as that which flowers / endlessly open into" (*Eighth Elegy*, 15–16) of which the animal is mirror, evidently recalls Dante's Flower. Animal and Angel appear *assured* in and of their space, appropriately disposed in it: nothing draws them into the future, no force can transcend their present. "Where we see Future, it sees Everything / itself in Everything, for ever healed" (*Eighth Elegy*, 41–42). The gaze of the animal enjoys the same autonomy from spatial fragmentation and temporal succession as that enjoyed by the angelical games in the Areopagite and Dante. Our gesture is opposed to the secured consistency (at the two poles of the axis mundi) of Angel and animal: that gesture of creatures forever about to leave, figures of the exodus, surprised in the instant in which they turn to take leave of their own earth: "we live our lives, for ever taking leave" (*Eighth Elegy*, 75). But the analogy hides an inexorable difference—and *that* is why the animal can be for us an image of the Angel; *that* is why its patibilis face can preserve for us a flutter of the Angel's wings. And this difference reverberates in the "safe" space of the Angel, overwhelming the necessity attributed to it by Dante. "And yet, within the wakefully warm animal / there lies the weight and care of a great sadness" (*Eighth Elegy*, 43–44), which the heavenly bee did not know about, but which the Angels of the two Gregories, the Theologian and the Nissene, as well as those of Narsai and Isaac of Nineveh knew all too well. The animal is also overtaken by this burden and anxiety that gush from the force that oppresses us: "die Erinnerung", memory, but understood as the faculty of becoming inward to oneself, and through this movement interiorizing in oneself the thing, transposing it into the invisible. The animal remembers and thus suffers a detachment from the earth, from the womb. It, too, is ex-pression; and this expression is irreversible. The silence of in–fancy is not sufficient to suppress expression. The Angel, instead, persists in its Rose, like "the gnat, that can still leap *within*, / even on its wedding-day" (*Eighth Elegy*, 54–55). The animal of Rilke, indeed, flies like the Angel, but it flies *away* and remembers from where. Memory constitutes the bridge between us and the animal, just as the direction of the gaze and the in–fancy constitutes that between animal and Angel. But we remember the Angel only through these stages: from the ou-topic image of a happy, complete forgetfulness to the "*little* creature" for which still "womb is all," to the "zigzags through the air / like crack through cup" of a bird flying "as though it were afraid / of its own self" (*Eighth Elegy*, 63–64), all the way down to the most miserable animal, forced to stay on the ground, bearing the weight of Erinnerung. The Angel lives through the passing away of these forms, by now connected forever to the uneasiness of our gaze, to the gesture of our farewell.

The Angel of the *Verkündigung* already prefigured the traits of this animal oppressed by the wave of our memory. It appeared, indeed, forgetful, but *thirsty*: it addressed us in order to drink from our features. This thirst dimmed its matutinal cognitio (knowledge). It had forgotten—but its forgetting was no longer perfect because it remembered, in front of She who medidates, that it had forgotten. And the forgotten dream (the annunciation of which was the reason for embarking on that journey; better, on that fall) burned its lips like a great thirst. Its cracked mirror already imagines that other crack which is the uncertain flight of the animal— and that wound which are our step and the "rhythm" of our saying.

Like the Angel, the animal also has a time that is not torn into past and future (a midrashic tale narrates that Gabriel was sent to grant eternal life to whomever would receive him for an instant. But the Angel returned and said: "They all had one foot in the past and the other in the future; I found no one who had the time"). But the animal remembers the past, carries it within, in its own being-mute. The animal's "aevum" arranges the different dimensions of time of which the Angel senses confusedly only the wave. But it is through the in–fant memory of the animal that we can imagine the Angel; it is through the pain, the melancholy of its face that we can imagine the Angel's face, which "announces" its own forgetfulness. The animal is our angel of the Angel. But will it still, in this its liminal figure, keep its gaze fixed straight ahead? Certainly, the animal moves into the Open, ins Freie—but will it also look to the Open? The animal is secure in its being-mute—but will it also see that silence opening before it, which it hears and drinks? The last stage of the animal, the closest one to us, even closer than the bird, only half secure, bears the sign of a face turned round. It remains in–fant, still flies into the

Open, but its face looks backward, having assumed the gesture of memory; it has interiorized the memory of the creature: starting with that of the Angel and ending with that of the most fleeting and ephemeral of creatures. Metamorphosis of the New Angel accomplished through the signs of the zodiac, and somehow destined ab origine by these very signs.

In its angelical aspect, this is Benjamin's figure; in its animal aspect, this is the world of Franz Marc. The "pure" animal of Marc *stands*, in its "great sadness" (the Sorge [sorrow] and Schwermut [melancholy] of Rilke), obedient to its necessity but comprehended in a light that it does not disfigure or poison or grasp in order to possess.[6] The "pure" animal is "secure" only in its own Sorge. It is the Angel of this necessity. Beside its icons riveted to the world (*Horse in Landscape*, 1910; *Dog facing the world*, drawing of 1911–1912; etc.), beside its cosmogonic transfigurations (*The cow of the world*, 1913), its "human" images make their entrance. And these all have their faces turned round. Its figure undergoes a painful torsion, it folds back onto itself in order to reflect and question itself (*Tiger*, 1912; *Deer in flower garden*, 1913; etc.). Suffering the Rilkean Erinnerung, the animal of Marc is also forced to turn against itself. It longs for the complete forgetfulness that even the Angel has forgotten, but by now it is captured in the act of remembering itself. And its memory knows a sorrow that was not experienced even by Gabriel in front of Mary. The animal still dwells in the Open but its eyes no longer look to it. It is suspended between the Open, which has become invisible also for it, and this necessity of flying away from every womb, of measuring only distances. Marc gets to the bottom of the kenosis of angelology that Rilke began. The necessity of the Angel coincides with this movement.

The figure of Benjamin seems to reflect on the knot that unites-divides Rilke's Angel and Marc's animal (the very last and the very newest reminder of the ou-topic plot that we have followed all along these pages). The Angelus Novus moves into the Open, with the face turned backward. A profane attention for what is destined to us, for our Geschichte, has turned it this way. A wind—ou-topic pneuma and spiritus—continues to draw it where origin and goal coincide. But this "ubi" is no longer reflected in the Angel's gaze. Now it is the perfect no-where. And only this loss or absence

permits the Angel to become the interpreter or, better, the forgetful figure, cipher, and device of the chain of our catastrophes.
Turned towards them, it carries them ins Freie. It redeems them,
frees them. It is not turned round simply to say farewell, but to
transpose in itself, toward the Open, the lost thing, the absence; to
save from the "whore 'Once upon a time'" the absent face of the
beloved.

A single trait of its ancient and triumphal icon seems to persist: the in–fancy. The song of the New Angel has no "developments," has no echoes; it no longer resonates like a full song.
Radically akin to "our own little strip of orchard," that *would be*
"ein reines Menschliches" ("a pure human"), where lovers *might*
"utter strange things in the midnight air" (*Second Elegy*, 37–38),
the hymn of the Angelus Novus is the sound itself of the instant;
better, of the source of the instant: of the Open that is the condition
of all sound.[7] To transpose the visible into the invisible means to
return it to this unattainable source. The *perfect* ephemeron of the
New Angel's song symbolically represents the originary Aleph,
where the sound of the thing and of the name is no longer dis-cursive, where it no longer pro-duces through succession and connection. And for this reason it is *herrlich* (glorious). *Herrlich* is this
very being-here (Hiersein) when it is "saved" in the instant of the
Angel's hymn, in the uselessness, gratuitousness and unproductiv-
ity of this instant that expects nothing and implores for nothing:
the instant that the Angel sought in vain among men. This is why
the New Angel still has to be called *Angel*. It does not move (like all
our "stories") from the invisible (understood as mere no-thing) to
the given thing, to manifestation, and to the prolongation into the
future of every manifestation, but from the dis-course of entities to
the invisible that is not nothing but rather the place in which they
are "saved." For sure, we speak, name, give opinions—but we can
try to say to the Angel, try to say according to the symbolical-
eschatological dimension of the name. We can try to say to the New
Angel that is the hermeneut-passage to the invisible: it draws there
without grasping or comprehending, it accompanies there without
possessing.

Marc's conception of his work follows this movement: "I saw
the image which breaks up in the eyes of the water-hen when it
submerges itself: the thousand rings that surround each little life,

the blue of the whispering skies that the lake drinks, the ecstatic emergence *into another place"* (my emphasis).[8] The zodiac of Marc is not an embankment for the suffering of the earth nor does it proceed from in–fancy to speech according to the motion in which we seem inexorably caught, but on the contrary, it moves from discourse to in–fancy, to the in–fant hymn of the New Angel. The Angel reflects in the pure instant of its hymn the word that it has seen overflowing our gaze, the memories that it has seen us succumb to, while it dragged us ins Freie. With Franciscan care and patience[9] it has collected in itself these words and memories. It always seems on the point of taking leave from our catastrophes, and it always carries them along. Its essence is identical to the sound that stretches, firm and heartrending at once, for all the final beats of the *Concert for Violin and Orchestra* (1935) of Alban Berg.[10] An extremely slow and pure tear, it reveals all our nostalgia for the invisible instant of the New Angel's hymn and all our mourning for the necessary repetition of its deaths.

NOTES

Chapter 1. Since the Days of Tobias

* [Mundus imaginalis is the supersensible world that lies between the sensible and the intelligible worlds; it can be perceived by the imaginative faculty, itself the intermediary organ between sensible perception and intellectual intuition.—Translator's note]

1. On the idea of the soul as ad-verbum (by-word) of the divine Word see Meister Eckhart, *Quasi stella matutina* in: *Meister Eckhart. Sermons and Treatises*, trans. M. O'C. Walshe (Rockport, MA: Element, 1991), vol. 2., p. 149.

2. One should not confuse the role of intermediary, of *metaxy*, with that of intercession. Therefore Luther emphasizes the fact that in the Scriptures Angels are never asked to intercede. However, he calls the figures of the Angel "cherished" and accepts the *blessing* that comes from them. In "On Translating: An Open Letter" (1530) he writes: "Even the patriarch Jacob did not ask the Angel with whom he wrestled for any intercession, but merely took from him the blessing." *Luther's Works*, ed. E. T. Bachmann (Philadelphia: Fortress Press, 1955), vol. 35, p. 199.

3. Pseudo-Dionysius the Areopagite summarizes this tradition in *De coelesti hierarchia*, IV, 180c: "Someone might claim that God has appeared himself and without intermediaries to some of the saints. But in fact it should be realized that scripture has clearly shown that 'no one has ever seen' or will ever see the being of God in all its hiddenness." (*The Celestial Hierarchy*, in *Pseudo-Dionysius: The Complete Works*, trans. Colm Luibheid [New York: Paulist Press, 1987]). J. Daniélou, in *Les Anges et leur mission d'après les Pères de l'Eglise* (Chevetogne, 1952), attempts to reconcile this principle with that held by Paul in Hebrews 11:6–9 where the communication of the Law by the Angels seems to be opposed to the

95

revelation of Christ. As we will see, the problem of angelic intercession is closely tied to the problem of their "speculating" power—that is, of their power *as mirrors*. On the divine mirror, which reflects Illum (That) for us, see the fundamental indications given by J. Baltrusaitis, *Le miroir* (Paris, 1978). But the theme of the mirror merges into the theme of the perfection of angelic legibility and so relates to the complex problem, to which we will return, of the Angel's language. J. Gerson speaks of Angels as the "mirrors or books of the most limpid images and writing."

4. See Leo Schaya, *The Universal Meaning of the Kabbalah* (Boston: Unwin Paperbacks, 1989).

5. These are Plotinian and generally Neoplatonic themes that are recovered by John Scot Eriugena and up to Schelling, whose *Weltalter*, in certain passages, seems to cite these words of Meister Eckhart: "God creates this entire world fully and totally in this present now. All that God created six thousand years ago and more, when he made the world, he creates right now and all together" (*Praedica verbum*, in *Meister Eckhart, Mystic and Philosopher*, trans. Reiner Schürmann [Bloomington: Indiana University Press, 1978], p. 181). Analogous themes are present in Sufi mysticism. Rumi, the great Rumi, whom Hegel cites at the end of the *Encyclopaedia* as the incomparable example of the soul's elevation over the finite and the vulgar, says: "At every instant the world renews itself and we are ignorant of its renewal, because it seems to us stable and eternal. Life propagates as an ever new torrent, yet, in our body, it seems continuous and unmoving" (Rumi, *The Mathnawi of Jalalu'dinn Rumi*, trans. R. A. Nicholson [London, 1977]).

6. Al-Suhrawardi, Yahya ibn Habash. *L'Archange empourpré. Quinze traités et récits mystiques*, trans. H. Corbin (Paris, Fayard, 1976), pp. 223–264.

7. Meister Eckhart, *Nunc scio vere* in *Meister Eckhart. Sermons and Treatise*, vol. 1, p. 198.

8. Florenskii in his *Ikonostas* (1922) (Italian translation: *Le porte regali. Saggio sull'icona*, ed. E. Zolla, [Milan, 1977]; pp. 53–55.) refers to the "inhabitants" of the temple, "intelligible place . . . topos noētos," as the "witnesses of the invisible," "angelical figures of the angelical world." An elementary guide to the iconology of the Angel is found in P. Lamborn Wilson, *Angels* (London, 1980). See also F. Saxl, *A Heritage of Images* (Harmondsworth: Penguin, 1970).

9. Fr. 1 and Fr. 16, *The Chaldean Oracles*, trans. Ruth Majercik (Leiden: E. J. Brill, 1989).

10. Proclus, *The Platonic Theology*, trans. Thomas Taylor [1816] (Kew Gardens, N.Y.: Selene Books, 1985).

11. On this point (as on numerous other aspects of our book), see L. Moraldi, *L'al di là dell'uomo nelle civiltà babilonese, egizia, greca, latina, ebraica, cristiana e musulmana* (Milan, 1985).

12. In the Christological domain, the Icon of the Angel has to be interpreted on the model of the Icon of the Son. The Son, in fact, is the *perfect Icon* of the Father, therefore it is *Invisible*, like the Father: "ita imaginem quoque invisibilem genuerit" ("He also begat an image that was invisible"). Origen, *De principiis*, I, 2, 6. (English translation: *On First Principles*, trans. Rev. F. Crombie, in *The Ante-Nicene Fathers* [Grand Rapids, Mich.: Eerdmans, 1951], vol. 4.)

13. In this respect, see the beautiful pages of Philo of Alexandria in *De Vita Mosis*, I, 66 (*Life of Moses*, in Colson ed. *Philo*, vol. 6, Loeb Classical Library [Cambridge, Mass.: Harvard University Press, 1950]) where in the center of the fire, in the center of the burning bush, he imagines a *morphē* (shape), an *agalma* (statue or image of worship) of the most splendid kind that "cannot be compared to any of the visible things." This figure-nonfigure, this invisible form of the Invisible, this *eikōn* (semblance) of He who is, "is called Angel."

14. "Gospel according to Philip," *Nag Hammadi Codex II, 2–7*, vol. 1, trans. W. Isenberg (Leiden: E. J. Brill, 1989).

15. See Plotinus, *Enneads* (VI, 9, 10), trans. Stephen MacKenna (New York: Pantheon Books, 1956).

16. This unification cannot occur in the domain of discursive knowledge, at none of its levels, since, even if it is true that "never did eye see the sun unless it had first become sunlike (helioeides), and never can the soul have vision of the First Beauty unless itself beautiful" (Plotinus, *Enneads*, I, 6, 9), still "it is right to deem light and vision sunlike, but never to think that they are the sun" (Plato, *Republic*, VI, 509a). The mystical exalts, renders "euphoric," the movement of resemblance until, in the discursively unattainable contemplation of Truth, the full henosis happens by grace: "God dwells in light supreme, no path can give access; / Yourself must be that light, if you would then progress" (Angelus Silesius, *The Cherubinic Wanderer*, I, 72, trans. M. Shrady [New York: Paulist Press, 1986]). Entirely Plotinian, instead, is Goethe in *Xenien*: "If the eye were not *sonnenhaft* [of the nature of the sun, participating of the sun] / how could we see the light?" Finally, Hölderlin in *Menschenbeifall* ("Human Applause"): "In gods and godhead only he can / Truly believe

who himself is godlike" (*Friedrich Hölderlin, Poems and Fragments*, trans. M. Hamburger [New York: Cambridge University Press, 1980], p. 47).

17. Iamblichus, *On the Mysteries*, English trans. A. Wilder (Hastings, England: Chthonios Books, 1989).

* [The author systematically writes *educare* (to educate) as *e-ducare* in order to emphasize the root of the word: *ducere*, Lat. "to lead." *E-ducare* then connotes a process of "leading out."—Translator's note]

18. Iamblichus, ibid., I, 8.

19. In particular, it develops the first chapter of the second part of my *Icone della Legge* (*Icons of the Law*) (Milan, 1985).

20. Moses Maimonides, *The Guide of the Perplexed*, II, 6, trans. Shlomo Pines (Chicago: University of Chicago, 1963).

21. This is how Hegel, in his *Lectures on the History of Philosophy*, interpreted the Alexandrian master, referring himself in particular to *De Opificio Mundi* and to the *Quaestiones et Solutiones in Genesim*, III, 11.

22. H. Corbin, *Nécessité de l'angélologie*, in *Le paradoxe du monothéisme* (Paris: éd. de L'Herne, 1981). This essay, in spite of the reservations that I will make explicit throughout, constitutes an incomparable synthesis of angelology.

23. The same theme is found in the "Gospel According to Philip" 53: 15–20, cited previously: "Light and darkness, life and death, right and left, are brothers of one another. They are inseparable. . . . Names given to the worldly are very deceptive for they divert our thoughts from what is correct to what is incorrect. . . . But truth brought names into existence in the world for our sakes because it is not possible to learn it without names."

24. On the apocalyptic thematic see the two interesting collections: *Apocalisse e ragione*, "Hermeneutica," 3, 1984; and *Tempo e Apocalisse*, ed. S. Quinzio (Milazzo, 1985), which includes essays by Mancini, Sartori, Givone and others. For an opposing interpretation (the whole of history is apocalypse, that is, revelation of Christ), see the essay by E. Corsini, *Apocalisse prima e dopo* (Turin, 1980); a work of great philosophical and conceptual vigor, although lacking a direct and explicit confrontation with contemporary orthodox eschatology (in particular that of Sergei Boulgakov), in other words, with its authentic antithesis.

25. And St. Augustine: ". . . etiam cum similes ei erimus, quando eum videbimus sicuti est . . . nec tunc natura illi erimus aequales," *De Trinitate*, XV, 16, 26 ("even when 'we shall be like to him', when 'we shall see him just as he is' . . . not even then shall we be equal to that nature" [*The Trinity*, trans. Stephen MacKenna; Fathers of the Church 45 (Washington, D.C.: Catholic University of America Press, 1963)]). The fundamental text regarding this question of *similitudo* seems to be 1 John 3:2, "*nunc* filii Dei sumus" ("we are God's children *now*"), what we shall be has yet to appear. When He will appear, then we shall be "similes ei" ("like Him"). Not even the eschatological vision shall make us equal. Meister Eckhart will push to its extreme consequences the problem of the difference between *similitudo* (likeness) and *aequalitas* (equality) (see *Expositio Evangelii secundum Johannem* ["Commentary on John"], 549).

26. C. Korvin Krasinski, *Microcosmo e macrocosmo nella storia delle religioni* (Milan, 1973).

27. Aimon d'Auxerre, quoted by H. de Lubac, *Exégèse médiévale*, Première Partie (Paris, 1959), vol. 2, p. 624.

28. English trans. H. M. Wilkins. *Expositions on The Book of Psalms*, in *Library of Fathers of the Holy Catholic Church*, vol. 5; (Oxford, 1853). See also *De Trinitate*, XV, 2, 2: "Non enim ait: laetetur cor invenientium; sed: quaerentium Dominum. . . . Et rursus intellectus eum quem invenit adhuc quaerit. . . ." ("Indeed, he does not say: let the heart of those rejoice who find; but rather: of those who seek the Lord. . . . And again the understanding still seeks Him whom it has found").

29. On the universal diffusion of the symbolism of the wings, see Mircea Eliade, "Symbolisms of Ascension and 'Waking Dreams'," in *Myths, Dreams and Mysteries* (New York: Harper, 1975).

30. For the translations of Dante's *Paradiso* and *Purgatorio* I refer to *The Divine Comedy*, trans. C. S. Singleton (Princeton, N.J.: Princeton University Press, 1977); for the translation of the *Inferno*, I refer to *The Divine Comedy*, trans. John D. Sinclair (New York: Oxford University Press, 1961).—Translator's note.

31. A. K. Coomaraswamy has called attention to the relation between these passages in Dante and the Oriental traditions in *Selected Papers* vol. 1, pp. 393, 453 (Princeton, 1977). He also quotes Rumi, *Divan*, XXIX and XLIV: "Fly, fly my bird towards your fatherland, for you have escaped from the cage and your feathers have bloomed." But the idea that the angelic movement is an image of freedom from the laws of locomo-

tion is a topos of angelology. "The initial gesture that Angels trace against the luminous background of the day consists in a separation and a loss of solidarity from the Earth, from the heaviness and horizontality of the ground" (A. Boatto, *Lo sguardo dal di fuori* [Bologna, 1981], p. 106). This idea is equally central in Swedenborg: in the spiritual world each appears to the other as soon as he *wants*, everything that happens does so through immediate changes of state, escaping the temporal flux. These are the pages of the "old metaphysician" that Ulrich transcribes "with a smile," at the end of his laborious attempt to clarify his ideas on the subject of the difference between the "definite feeling," always "with arms outstretched to grasp something," and the "indeterminate" *Stimmung* (mood), the calm without appetite, the "interior world" (R. Musil, *Ulrich und die zwei Welten des Gefühls*, in *Aus dem Nachlass, Gesammelte Werke*, [Hamburg, 1978], vol. 4, pp. 1202–1203).

* [The author will often write *ad-tendere* instead of *attendere* (to wait, to expect) to play with the idea that in all waiting there is a "stretching" (*tendere*) "toward" (*ad*). Depending on context, I use both *to attend* and *to wait*.—Translator's note]

32. *The Book of Jubilees*, in *The Apocrypha and Pseudepigrapha of the Old Testament*, ed. R. H. Charles (Oxford: Clarendon Press, 1973), vol. 2.

33. *Hekhalot Rabbati*, in *I Sette Santuari*, ed. A. Ravenna and E. Piattelli (Turin, 1964); G. Scholem, *Major Trends in Jewish Mysticism* (New York: Schocken Books, 1961); L. Schaya, *The Universal Meaning of the Kabbalah*.

34. For a brief but precise introduction to Islamic angelology, see T. Fahd, *Anges, démons, et djinns en Islam,* in *Génies, anges et démons* (Paris, 1971). The author is particularly insistent on the significance of the angelic "plenum" of the heavenly spaces (p. 162).

35. English translation in Rainer Maria Rilke, *Duino Elegies*, trans. J. B. Leishman and Stephen Spender (New York: W. W. Norton and Co., 1963); also in *Letters of Rainer Maria Rilke*, trans. J. B. Greene and M. D. H. Norton (New York: W. W. Norton and Co., 1945–1948).

36. The trilogy of mystical tales by Avicenna (*The Recital of Hayy ibn Yaqzan*; *The Recital of the Bird*; *Recital of Salaman and Absal*) has been studied, commented on, and translated by H. Corbin, *Avicenna and*

the Visionary Recital, trans. W. R. Trask (Princeton, N.J.: Princeton University Press, 1990).

* [The author uses the Italian *principio*, which means both "beginning" and "principle."—Translator's note]

37. Ibn 'Arabi, *Trajuman al-shwaq. The Interpreter of Desires*, ed. R. A. Nicholson (London, 1911). On Ibn 'Arabi, see H. Corbin, *Creative Imagination in the Sufism of Ibn 'Arabi*, trans. R. Manheim (Princeton, N.J.: Princeton University Press, 1969). It is the "God who has neither shape nor form but sits enthroned above the Intellectual-Principle (*Nous*) and all the Intellectual-sphere (*Noëton*)," which Plotinus could attain only four times in his life (Porphyry, *Life of Plotinus*, 23; English trans. Stephen MacKenna, *Enneads*).

38. "I myself will send an angel before you . . . my name is in him" (Exodus 23: 20–21). In the Angel is found the "shem" of Yahweh: the Angel is not the name of God, but it carries it within and offers it.

39. See the introduction by P. Isotta to G. Locchi, *Wagner, Nietzsche e il mito sovrumanista* (Rome, 1982), p. 11.

40. See the fundamental research of R. Hammerstein, *Die Musik der Engel* (Bern and Munich, 1962); and *Die Musik in Dantes Divina Commedia*, "Deutsches Dante-Jahrbuch," 41–42, 1964.

41. These verses of *Purgatory* have furnished the title and the central idea to the important work of H. Kayser, *Bevor die Engel sangen. Eine harmonikale Anthologie* (Basel, 1953).

42. Such music is opposed by Satanic music, whose culmination is *absolute silence*, the desertlike absence of voice that reigns at the bottom of Hell. This absolute silence is symmetrically opposed to the unimaginable Ineffable that concludes Paradise. God dwells "in excelsis in silentio," (in the heights, in silence) St. Augustine, *Confessions*, I, 1, 18–19. The universe seems to be embraced by these two silences. On Satanic music, see R. Hammerstein, *Diabolus in Musica* (Bern and Munich, 1974), which completes the investigations on the iconography and conception of medieval music in *Die Musik der Engel*.

43. Like the one Henry Corbin attempts to establish in the last pages of *Philosophie iranienne et philosophie comparée* (Tehran, 1977). The "mistake" of Corbin (which is occasioned by an all too "seductive" assertion made by Rilke himself) is fully shared not only by critics and histori-

ans of literature, but also by philosophers like H. -G. Gadamer: "the Rilke expert realizes immediately that the Plotinian spirit inspired the vision of angels of the *Elegies* of Duino" (*Denken als Erlösung. Plotin zwischen Plato und Augustin* in H. -G. Gadamer, *Gesammelte Werke*, vol. 7 [Tübingen: Mohr, 1991]).

44. F. Jesi, *Esoterismo e linguaggio mitologico. Studi su Rainer Maria Rilke* (Messina and Florence, 1976), has mentioned Rilke's attraction to Russian religiosity without engaging the specific problem of angelology.

45. [For Rilke's *Duino Elegies* I refer to the English translation by J. B. Leishman and Stephen Spender. On occasion, Cacciari's translation diverges from the English one, in which cases I have followed Cacciari's version.—Translator's note]

46. "Ange plein de gaieté, connaissez-vous l'angoisse, / La honte, les remords, les sanglots, les ennuis / Et les vagues terreurs de ces affreuses nuits / Qui compriment le coeur comme un papier qu'on froisse?" ("Angel of gaiety, have you tasted grief? / Shame and remorse and sobs and weary spite, / And the vague terrors of the fearful night / That crush the heart up like a crumpled leaf?") Baudelaire, *Réversibilité* [English trans., "Reversibility" in *The Flowers of Evil* trans. F. P. Sturm (New York: New Directions, 1955).]

47. "The descending chain having been interrupted, not even eros-nostalgia can climb any higher. This is why there no longer exists a continuity between the beautiful and the glorious, which now can only appear as terrifying," H. U. von Balthasar, *The Realm of Metaphysics in the Modern Age*, in *The Glory of the Lord*, vol. V, (San Francisco: Ignatius Press, 1991). But later Balthasar asserts that Angels, because of this breach that occurred between God and nature, now could represent only an indeterminable *x*. According to me, instead, it is precisely out of this breach that the new names of the Angel, also in Rilke, originate.

48. From Pseudo-Dionysius to Meister Eckhart the tradition remains univocal on this point. See Meister Eckhart, *Missus est Gabriel angelus* in *Meister Eckhart. Sermons and Treatises*, vol. 1, p. 211. The Angel, in as much as it is *Kērux*, Messenger, is profoundly linked to the whole dimension of the *kērygma* (proclamation) of the Annunciation. See G. Kittel, *Theologische Wörterbuch zum Neuen Testament*, III, 682.

49. This represents the fundamental theme (from Collosians 2:18) evoked in the works of Corbin to explain the progressive disappearance of angelology in Christianity. It seems to me that one can speak of such a

phenomenon only with several distinctions and reservations, and in any case not before the fourteenth or fifteenth century. Is it possible, for example, to separate the theological syntheses from the great medieval figurative representations? Can the angelical presence in the two major *events* of the life of Christ, Birth and Ascension, be interpreted only as a ritual and passive participation? Did not the Church Fathers assert that the advent of Christ *reinforced* the angelical ministry, allowing it to overcome the great crisis that had torn it apart in the moment of the creation of man? And the angelical *stupor* before the Incarnation, stupor before the elevation of human nature over the angelical worlds themselves, does this not figure a *dramatourgia* (drama) that is far more complex and tormented than what appears in Corbin's critique? On these issues, see H. de Lubac, *Corpus mysticum* (Paris, 1949); J. Daniélou, *Las Anges et leur mission d'après les Pères de l'Eglise.*

50. Rilke, *Puppen,* in *Werke* (Frankfurt am Main, 1980), vol. 3, book 2; p. 538. English trans., Graig Houston, "Some Reflections on Dolls," in *Selected Works* (London: Hogarth Press, 1954), vol. 1, p. 46.

51. On the days of Tobias, on the guardian Angel, on the nostalgia that we have always borne for it, see the very beautiful pages in Eugenio D'Ors, *Introducción a la vida ángelica* [1939], (Madrid, 1980). Bygone are those days when the Angel was clearly recognizable as our heavenly alter ego, symbol of the astral body, perfect superior vehicle (*ochēma*) "in which the demiurge has placed the soul," H. Corbin, *Spiritual Body and Celestial Earth: From Mazdean Iran to Shiite Iran,* (Princeton, N.J.: Princeton University Press, 1977). For a long time, Christian angelology has vacillated on the problem of the astral body of the Angel. It is only with St. Thomas Aquinas that all hylomorphism is rejected. St. Bonaventure still preached the composition "ex materia et forma" ("out of matter and form") of the Angel.

52. "All creatures are green in God," but the foliage of the great Tree of creation is the Angel. Meister Eckhart, *Videns Jesus Turbas* in *Meister Eckhart. Sermons and Treatises,* vol. 2, p. 327.

53. The excessive and de-lirious character of our epoch is one of the constant themes in Nietzsche (see aphorism 374 of *The Gay Science*). It resonates in Rilke together with the other Nietzschean theme of the "new justice," of *Gerechtigkeit*: to do justice to the thing, to preserve the rythmos (measured motion) of presence and of unconcealment, the rythmos of the tragic polemos (conflict) engraved in the Anaximander fragment.

54. See H. Corbin, *Temple and Contemplation* (New York, 1986).

55. From 2 Timothy 4:2, and it signifies: "Proclaim the word, pronounce it, produce it, and beget the word" (Meister Eckhart, *Praedica verbum*, trans. Schürmann, p. 181).

56. On the opposition between chronological time and mystical time, see M. de Certeau, *The Mystic Fable*, trans. M. B. Smith (Chicago: University of Chicago Press, 1992). The vast research of M. de Certeau, although not directly engaged with angelological problems, is fundamental to the ends of our essay. It documents, among other things, the persistence of angelological themes in the constitution of the mystical "science" in the sixteenth and seventeenth centuries.

57. Meister Eckhart, *Praedica verbum*, trans. Schürmann, p. 182.

58. Meister Eckhart, *Ave, gratia plena*, in *Meister Eckhart. Sermons and Treatises*, vol. 2, p. 61. According to Athanagoras, God is eternally and intrinsically Logikos: the Son is his name. Similarly in the gnostic Gospels (See "The Gospel of Truth," *Nag Hammadi Codices I, 3,* [Leiden: E. J. Brill, 1991]).

* [*Erinnerung*, the German term for "memory, remembrance"; the author systematically spells it *Er-innerung* to emphasize the connotations of a process of interiorization.—Translator's Note]

59. Meister Eckhart, *Praedica verbum*, trans. Schürmann, p. 181.

60. The presence of angelological themes in the work of the philosophus teutonicus, on whose account, as Hegel will say, "we should not blush," is extremely vast. At least ten chapters of *Aurora consurgens* treat this subject. And even though Jakob Boehme did not recognize completely the validity of this, his first book ("I warn the reader who loves God that this book of Dawn has not been completed, because the devil has obstructed it, recognizing that thanks to it the day was about to dawn"), his angelological vision remains nearly unchanged in *Mysterium Magnum*. For *Aurora* see the French translation by A. Koyré, in *La philosophie de Jacob Boehme*, (Paris: Vrin, 1971).

61. These are well-known Heideggerian etymologies and interpretations. It seems to me that the whole of Heidegger's oeuvre, at least since *The Origin of the Work of Art*, through *The Anaximander Fragment*, up to the essays of *The Question Concerning Technology*, can be conceived as a radical rethinking of the Rilkean Dichtung (poetry), in particular of his *Duino Elegies*, filtered through continuous citations of the High German mystical language.

* [The author renders the Italian term *ricordare* (to remember) as *ri-cor-dare*, which can be construed as "to give back by heart, from the heart."—Translator's note]

62. But how to believe in the pertinence of such a term if one has seen the Trinity of Andrej Rublëv? Such powerful images—where manifestation and mystery, apparition and impenetrable Aidōs are combined in an indissoluble harmony—must also enter into the scope of angelological investigation, into the *thought* of the Angel. Without these images every theology remains a dead letter. Actually, not even at the culmination of the Roman Baroque does the image of the Angel appear completely triumphal. This reference is not as strange as it may seem if one thinks of the influence exerted on Bernini by the Areopagitic writings, published anew in 1634 in a Latin translation and bearing an etching by Rubens on their title page (R. Wittkower, *G. L. Bernini. The Sculptor of the Roman Baroque* [London, 1981]). Bernini's "angelology" is much more complex than might appear at first sight. The powerful Angel that draws the Canopy of St. Peter "upward" is not the same as the leitourgika pneumata (ministering spirits) of the Cappella del Sacramento and is even less similar to the Angels of Passion of the Ponte Sant'Angelo. The one with the crown of thorns is virile, heroic; whereas the one with the scroll ornament is delicate, lyrical—but both participate in the Passion, and are not absorbed by the immutable bliss, by the smile without shadow of the heavenly choirs. The vortices of their robes comprise dramatic evidence of the sort of whirlwind that has wrenched them down here. To those Angels that guard St. Peter's Chair or adore the Tabernacle or participate in the Passion—Angels always represented in the full flower of years—the adolescent figures suspended in a hermaphroditic limbo form a counterpoint. These appear to us in a closer relation to humans: they bring them messages (like the Angel does to Habakkuk, in the Chigi chapel at Santa Maria del Popolo), they strike them with the arrow of divine love (the famous Saint Theresa of the Coronaro chapel at Santa Maria della Vittoria). And in this latter 'role' their smile merges with that of a pagan Eros and the ecstasis is transformed into a "sweet languishing" (as the contemporaries already understood). Even here, then, where its figure most should have had to exalt the scene of an unchangeable triumph, the Angel appears "in danger" (and therefore periculosum-terrifying!), with a living and changeable countenance.

63. Rilke, *The Book of Images*, trans. E. Snow (San Francisco: North Point Press, 1991).

64. Rilke, *Verstreute und nachgelassen Gedichte aus dem Jahren 1906–1926*, in *Werke*, vol. 2, book 1, p. 71. English translation by J. B. Leishman, *Poems 1906 to 1926* (New York: New Directions, 1957).

65. That such a movement is much more complex than the "simple disappearance of God" behind an angelical figure that by now belongs to our world (R. Guardini, *Rainer M. Rilke* [Munich, 1961]) is what should now appear as evident.

Chapter 2. Angel and Demon

1. According to Origen, men originate from the uncertain Angels, those who in the supreme instant of decision sided neither with God nor with Satan. On Origen's angelology, see M. Simonetti, "Due note sull'angelologia Origeniana," *Rivista di cultura classica e medievale* 4, no. 2, (1962). The motif of man as an irresolute Angel will be recovered by the hermetic Neoplatonism of humanism, see E. Wind, "The Revival of Origen," in *The Eloquence of Symbols. Studies in Humanist Art* (Oxford, 1983); and, always in the domain of iconological research, J. Seznec, *La Survivance des anciens dieux* (Paris, Flammarion).

* [*Drān*: Greek term for action, in the sense of an irrevocable decision, of a unique responsibility towards one's *daimon*, wrenched from determinism and the network of causal relations.—Translator's note]

2. On the theme of polyophtalmy, see R. Pettazzoni, *L'essere supremo nelle religioni primitive* (Turin, 1974).

3. *The Gospel of Bartholomew* III, 54–55, in *New Testament Apocrypha*, vol. 1, ed. W. Schneemelcher (Louisville, Ky.: John Knox Press, 1991).

4. The rivalry between Iblis (Satan) and Adam constitutes one of the fundamental aspects of Islamic demonology. The shaytan of the Koran is not the adversary of God but of man, because man was the one "chosen" by God; see T. Fahd, *Anges, démons et dijnns en Islam*, pp. 175–180. The motivations for such "jealousy" are strictly *theological*: Iblis is the greatest martyr-witness to the unique and inaccessible essence of God. It was this pure, simple and unshareable essence that it proclaimed to the Angels. The great mystic Husayn Mansur Hallaj establishes a relation between this jealous monotheism of Satan, who cannot tolerate the thought that God "resembles" the material and humble form of Adam, and Muhammad's hesitation at the threshold of the divine fire, hesitation

at consuming himself in that fire to become one with the Burning Bush, with the object of his love. Must not the Light of the One be safeguarded in its incommunicability? Does not mystical love, which tends toward the identification with its proper object, necessarily appear impure in relation to the "absolute" praise that Satan elevates toward the Unattainable?

5. Different testimony in Job 38:7, where the Angels greet the creation with jubilation.

6. *The Apocalypse of Paul* (10), in *New Testament Apocrypha*, vol. 2.

7. The biblical story is also recalled in the Gnostic *Apocryphon of John* (29:17–20), where the Old Testament demiurge, Ialdabaoth, sends his angels-archons "to the daughters of mankind to take some of them unto themselves and so to raise up a posterity," in *The Gnostic Scriptures*, trans. Bentley Layton (Garden City, N.Y.: Doubleday Books, 1987).

8. G. Scholem, *Major Trends in Jewish Mysticism* (New York: Schocken Books, 1954), p. 67.

9. "Un Ange, imprudent voyageur / qu'a tenté l'amour du difforme" ("An angel, rash wanderer, who craves to look upon deformity"), Baudelaire, *L'Irrémédiable* [English translation. "The Irremediable," in *Flowers of Evil*].

10. On biblical demonology, see E. Dhorme, *La démonologie biblique*, in *Mélanges*, (Montpellier, France: W. Vischer, 1960). A. Rosenberg, *Engel und Daimonen*, (Munich, 1866). For a brief summary of postbiblical angelology and demonology, see C. Gonzalo Rubio, *La angelología en la literatura rabínica y sefardí* (Barcelona, 1977). But see above all Riwkah Schärf, *The Figure of Satan in the Old Testament*, in C. G. Jung, *La Simbolica dello Spirito*, Italian translation, (Turin, 1959). This text demonstrates the peculiarity of Satan with respect to the pagan demon; namely, the eminently spiritual character of its function of seduction.

11. For a commentary and study of the sources of these passages in Philo, I refer to the introduction and notes of R. Radice, in Philo of Alexandria, *Le origini del male* (Milan, 1984). See also J. -P. Vernant, *Myth and Thought Among the Greeks* (Boston: Routledge, 1983); L. Thorndike, *A History of Magic and Experimental Science*, vol. 1 (New York, 1923), remains indispensable.

12. In the *Apocryphon of John*, already cited, it is the Demiurge along with his Angels-archons that creates Heimarmenē, the chain of Necessity. His Angels—one for each day of the year—protect it unfailingly.

13. G. Reale, *Saggio introduttivo* to Proclus, *I manuali. Elementi di fisica. Elementi di teologia*, ed. C. Faraggina (Milan, 1985).

14. For some further development of the decisive theme of insomnia, see my article "Tradizione e Storia," *il Centauro* 13–14 (1985). On the Angels that wake, see Judah Halevi, *Diwan*, éd. de L'éclat (Montpellier, France, 1988).

15. On the relation between angelical life and monasticism, see C. Korvin Krasinski, *Microcosmo macrocosmo . . .* , pp. 317ff.

16. Among the Church Fathers, it is Isaac of Nineveh who has insisted the most on the limits, the "incompleteness," of the figure of the Angel. See P. Bettiolo's introduction to Isaac of Nineveh, *Discorsi spirituali. Capitoli della conoscenza* (Bose, Italy, 1985).

17. Narsai, *Homélies sur la création*, ed. P. Gignoux, Patrologia Orientalis 34, 3-4, 1968, pp. 369–384. Therefore St. Paul's words, repeated by Dante in the Canto XXIV, 64–65, of *Paradiso* ("Faith is the substance of things hoped for and the evidence of things not seen"), could apply also to Angels. But this motif, as we will see, does not fit in with the eternal fixity of the direction of the Angel's gaze in Dante.

18. How much of this trait is present in Kafka's guardians? To what extent do they represent the last, self-evanescent gleam of the pure "gods of the instant?"

19. On the symbolism of colors in angelology, apart from P. Lamborn Wilson, *Angels*, see H. Corbin, *Nécessité de l'angélologie*, in *Le Paradoxe du monothéisme*; and P. Florenskii, *La colonna e il fondamento della verità*, ed. P. Modesto and E. Zolla (Milan, 1974), pp. 612ff.

20. Rilke, *Gedichte in französicher Sprache*, in *Werke*, vol. 2, book 2, p. 569. [*The Complete French Poems of Rainer Maria Rilke*, trans. A. Poulin (St. Paul, Minn.: Greywolf Press, 1986].

21. I quote from the extraordinary page in Kafka's *Diaries* of June 25, 1914. F. Kafka, *Tagebücher 1910–1923*, in *Gesammelte Werke*, ed. Max Brod, (Frankfurt, 1983), pp. 294–296; English translation, F. Kafka, *The Diaries 1910–1923*, ed. Max Brod, trans. Martin Greenberg and Hannah Arendt (New York: Schoken Books 1976).

22. The "passage" and the patience of the Angel are thematized in Walter Benjamin's fragment, *Agesilaus Santander*, which Scholem has presented and interpreted in "Walter Benjamin und sein Engel," in *Zur Aktualität Walter Benjamin* (Frankfurt am Main, 1972); English trans., "Walter Benjamin and His Angel," in *On Walter Benjamin*, ed. G. Smith (Cambridge, Mass.: MIT Press, 1991).

23. The meshes of the physico-mechanical world "are too wide, and through these escapes the specific singularity, the determinate individuality—the 'real'" (V. Vitiello, *Ethos ed eros in Hegel e Kant* [Naples, 1984], p. 45). This important work, which ends with the Rilkean image of the Angel, constitutes one of the constant theoretical references of this book.

24. The "irrevocability" of the terrestrial in Rilke is a theme already found in Hölderlin and Kleist, whom Rilke reads from a Nietzschean perspective.

25. On the iconology of the musician Angel, apart from the investigations by Hammerstein cited earlier, see E. Winternitz, *Musical Instruments and Their Symbolism in Western Art*, (New Haven, Conn.: Yale University Press, 1979).

26. "The heavens, the heavenly bodies . . . are either evil beings, or the seat of inferior Entities, such as the Demiurge and creator angels, or the seat of demonic Oppressors with bestial forms. . . . Man suffocates therein like in a prison" (Henri-Charles Puech, *En quête de la gnose*, Paris, Gallimard, 1978). The desperate struggle by the allogenes, by the "stranger," to flee the "starry heavens populated by oppressors and despots" (ibid.), to strike those "gentlemen astrologers" who, "like parrots in a cage," describe circles and spheres (Giordano Bruno, "Proemiale epistola," *De l'infinito, universo e mondi*), this very struggle is still at the center of the works, in themselves very different, of Florenskii and Shestov (see in particular Shestov's *Athens and Jerusalem* [Athens: Ohio University Press, 1966]). On the problem of Destiny in Antiquity, see G. de Santillana, *Fato antico e Fato moderno* (Milan, 1985), which nonetheless does not treat the theme, central for us, of angelology in its relation to demonology.

27. The daimon would be the link between the absolutely universal dimension of destiny and the particular human and divine figure, hence its relation to "character" or to "lineage" (daimon genthlios). K. W. F. Solger, in his essay *Über den Ursprung der Lehre von Dämonen und Schutzgeistern in der Religion der alten Griechen*, collected in *Nachgelassen Schriften und Briefwechsel* [1826] (Heidelberg, 1973),

specifies that the daimon attains this mediating role only to the extent that Greek Anangkē is not expressed in a unilateral fashion by its mechanistic-deterministic aspect, but rather as "anima mundis" (world soul).

28. This theme is amply developed by Apuleius in *De deo Socratis* (English trans. in *The Works of Apuleius*, London 1911). What would happen "if men were entirely removed from the immortal gods" (V, 129)? To whom and why should one pray? If nature is *dirempt* into a human nature and a divine nature, if, on the one side, only the ineffable greatness of the Father is knowable by intuition, and, on the other side, we have only the experience of the "miserable life" of man, then we have a better chance to be understood by a stone than by Zeus (V, 132). But between the supreme Aether and the miserable earth there exist "intermediary divine powers," which the Greeks call *demons*. They appear to Apuleius as vessels "in the sea of the air." Through these vessels we can communicate with the divine, because the demon "partakes" of our nature through its ingenium (intelligence) and its passions, but belongs to the nature of the Divine through its immortality. "Demons are as to genus animated beings, as to mind rational [ingenio rationabilia], as to feelings passive as to body aerial, as to duration eternal" (XIII, 148). In Apuleius the demon is benevolent a true guardian angel: "[it] sees all things, understands all things, and dwells in the most profound recesses of the mind, in the place of conscience" (XVI, 156), nonetheless the problem of the "reduction" of the demon to the faculty of the soul itself, to which we will return, is manifestly present.

29. See M. Detienne, "Sur la démonologie de l'ancien pythagorisme," *Revue d'Histoire des Religions* 155 (1959).

30. E. Rohde, *Psyche; The Cult of Souls and Belief in Immortality Among the Greeks* (Freeport, N.Y., 1972).

31. D. Del Corno, "Introduzione" to Plutarch, *Il demone di Socrate*. See also U. Bianchi, *La religione greca* (Turin 1975), p. 163.

32. E. Rohde, *Psyche*. For a more general development of these soteriological themes, see U. Bianchi, *Prometeo, Orfeo, Adamo* (Rome 1976), pp. 129–187; and, from a very different perspective, J. -P. Vernant, *Myth and Thought Among the Greeks*.

33. Although one could affirm along with Shestov ("Speculation and Apocalypse," in *Speculation and Revelation* [Athens: Ohio University Press, 1982]), in his radical critique of the philosophy of religion of Solovyev, that the Angel's function as guide ends up being nothing more than a metaphor of the "mens ducente ratione" (mind-guiding reason).

The Angel, then, would extricate itself from the relation to the demon only to fall prey to a "Hellenized" rationalistic teleology. Undoubtedly these are the two, complementary and opposite, poles of traditional angelology: uninterrupted oscillation between astral necessity and reassuring philosophical hermeneutics. The astral motif, though, has experienced disturbing and powerful returns in the "nocturnal face" of Modernity. T. Fechner, "the great Fechner" as Freud called him, the founder of contemporary psychophysics, writes on the subject of the earth in *Über die Seelenfrage* [1861]: "it is an Angel that moves through the sky ... and drags me in its bosom." On the importance of Fechner, and the emblematic character of his figure, see J. Hillman, *The Dream and the Underworld* (New York: Harper and Row, 1979); see also the preface by C. Rabant in *Anatomie comparée des Anges*, éd. de L'éclat, (Montpellier, France, 1987). Analogous considerations could be made for Louis-Auguste Blanqui's *L'Eternité par les astres* [1872], which so interested Walter Benjamin.

34. Aristotle remarks in *De Anima* (I, 5, 410b) that in the Orphic chants the soul, transported by the wind, penetrates beings as they breathe.

35. For a linguistical analysis of the problem, see E. Benveniste, *Indo-European Language and Society*, Miami Linguistics Series 12 (Miami: University of Miami Press, 1973). For a philosophical interpretation of Benveniste, see E. Severino, *Destino della necessità* (Milan, 1980). On the question of Daimon-Anangkē, see the vast research of Magris, *Idee del destino nel pensiero antico*, 2 vols. (Udine, 1984).

36. P. M. Schuhl, *Essais sur la formation de la pensée grecque* (Paris, 1949). *Anax*, sovereign, is the *theos ti* (the what that is god), the god who guides Agammenon's ship in Aeschylus—*anax* is the "god of place" invoked by Ulysses when he is cast on the shores of Schería. On the daimon in Homer, see M. Untersteiner, *Scritti Minori* (Brescia, 1971). Even though unstable and undetermined—or, rather, precisely because of this—the daimon is an overwhelming and inexorable lord. The Olympian gods (one should note that only Zeus and Apollo, among these gods, are called *anax* by Homer), at the apogee of their form, will have to interiorize its power: *Zeus kerauneios* (Zeus wielding the thunderbolt): "Thunderbolt [keraunos] steers all things" (Heraclitus, 64 DK). See E. R. Dodds, *The Greeks and the Irrational* (Berkeley: University of California Press, 1973); with regard to this famous book, see the pertinent criticisms of U. Bianchi, *La religione greca*.

37. Walter Benjamin, *Theses on the Philosophy of History,* in *Illuminations,* trans. H. Zohn and ed. H. Arendt (New York: Schocken Books, 1968).

38. G. Leopardi, *Elogio degli uccelli,* in *Operette morali,* ed. C. Galimberti (Naples, 1986); English trans. by G. Cecchetti (Berkeley: University of California Press, 1982). C. Galimberti has grasped with much intelligence and subtlety the angelological elements of the *Elogio.*

39. On the Angel in the contemporary world, the most complete investigation is found in J. Jiménez, *El ángel caído,* (Barcelona, 1982).

40. J. Jiménez, ibid., p. 139.

41. "Ich trage seinen grossen Flügel / Gebrochen schwer am Schulterblatt. . . ." ("For, broken at the shoulder blade, / I hear his wings' gigantic spans"), Else Laske-Schüler, *Gebet,* in *Gedichte, Gesammelte Werke,* vol. 1, (Munich: Kösel-Verlag, 1959). English trans., R. P. Newton, "Prayer," in *Your Diamond Dreams Cut Open My Arteries. Poems by Else Laske-Schüler* (Chapel Hill: University of North Carolina Press, 1982); p. 243.

42. "Von Sternen sind wir eingerahmt / und flüchten aus der Welt / Ich glaube wir sind Engel" ("We are framed by stars / And flee out of the world / I believe we are angels"), Else Laske-Schüler, *An den Graalprinzen,* ibid.

43. A clear separation between these two principles cannot be maintained, just like between light and darkness in *Les Chants de Maldoror,* during the struggle of Maldoror with the Angel. The theme of the gaze into the invisible appears also in Rilke's *The Notebooks of Malte Laurids Brigge.* The figure of Erik Brahe, who belongs to the world of the living thanks to his "healthy" eye, and to the invisible world of the dead that he looks into with his fixed eye, will be recovered by Rilke in the *Fourth Elegy,* 30–35. These themes have been carefully analysed by F. Pirani, "L'immagine angelica in Licini e Klee," diss. thesis, Rome, 1983.

44. The dialectic between Angel and Orpheus will be further developed by Cocteau in his cinematographical version of *Orpheus* (1950).

45. On this figure of the mirror, see G. Agamben, *Stanzas: Word and Phantasm in Western Culture,* trans. R. L. Martinez (Minneapolis: University of Minnesota Press, 1993). More generally, on the relations between imagination and representation, G. Carchia, *Estetica ed erotica* (Milan, 1981). I would also refer to my "Narciso o della pittura," *Spazio umano* 7 (1983).

46. P. Valéry, *L'Ange* [1945], in *Oeuvres* (Paris, 1957), vol. 1, pp. 205–206; English trans., Hilary Corke, *Paul Valéry, An Anthology* (Princeton, N.J.: Princeton University Press, 1977).

47. S. Solmi, *Meditazioni sullo Scorpione*, in *Opere* (Milan, 1984), vol. 1, pp. 14–16.

48. On the theme of infancy, see G. Agamben, *Infancy and History*, trans. L. Heron (New York: Verso, 1993).

49. Preserved in the human words, like the Gnostic Angels of the *Excerpta ex Theodoto*, 35, which, having exited the pleroma, having emerged from the One, will be able to return only after collecting the spiritual sparks dispersed down here. To this end they pray for us, awaiting their own return.

Chapter 3. The Problem of Representation

1. Walter Benjamin, "Schicksal und Charakter," in *Gesammelte Schriften* (Frankfurt: Suhrkamp, 1980), vol. 2, pt. 1, p. 175; English translation, E. Jephcott, trans., "Fate and Character," in *Reflections* (New York: Schocken Books, 1986).

2. The theme (which is found already in Schelling and Hölderlin) of the end of demonic destiny, of the *Übermacht* (overpowering) of destiny, is also central in the *Star of Redemption* by Franz Rosenzweig. To the figure of the "servant of God," simple subject of the *judgment* that destiny pronounces, is opposed, for the sake of man and the world, the "light of revelation." By its grace, the direction of the will is not demonically fixed once and for all, "but in every instant dies and in every instant is renewed" (F. Rosenzweig, *Der Stern der Erlösung*, 2d ed. [Frankfurt: Suhrkamp Verlag, 1930], pt. 2, book 3, pp. 160–163; English translation, William Hallo, trans., *The Star of Redemption* [New York: Holt, Rinehart, and Winston, 1971]). It would be of great interest in this respect to develop the analysis of the relation—to this day only mentioned in passing—between Benjamin and Aby Warburg. "The struggle with the monster" ("der Kampf mit dem Monstrum"), the exceedingly dangerous and never definitely overcome passage from the "monstruous complex to the ordering symbol" ("vom monströsen Komplex zum ordnenden Symbol") (quoted in H. Gombrich, *Aby Warburg* [London: The Warburg Institute, 1970], pp. 251–252), the capacity to safeguard-save the past by dominating its immediate demonic appearance—all the "polarities" of Warburg's genius are profoundly related to Benjamin's concept of character. "Homo

victor," one could say with Warburg (see ibid., p. 322), is he who "remains in control of his powers, man enough to blast open the continuum of history" (Walter Benjamin, "Theses on the Philosophy of History," XVI, in *Illuminations*, p. 262).

3. Ibid.

4. F. W. J. Schelling, *Philosophie der Kunst*, in *Sämmtliche Werke* (Stuttgart, 1856–1861), vol. 1, pt. 5, p. 697.

5. G. Colli, *La nascita della filosofia* (Milan: Adelphi, 1975), p. 67.

* [The author translates into Italian the German play of words: *zugrundegehen* (to perish) and *zu Grunde gehen* (to get to the bottom of something, to seek a foundation).—Translator's note]

6. The following quotations of Benjamin are taken from *Ursprung des deutschen Trauerspiels*, in *Gesammelte Schriften*, vol. 1, pt. 1, pp. 203ff; English translation, John Osborne, trans., *The Origin of German Tragic Drama* (London: New Left Books, 1977).

7. On the distance separating philosophy from "research" see the interesting pages in M. Sgalambro, *La morte del sole* (Milan: Adelphi, 1982).

8. The absence of any real gnostic influences in Benjamin has been clearly indicated both by F. Desideri, *Il tempo e le forme* (Rome: Armando, 1980), and by G. Schiavoni, *Walter Benjamin. Sopravvivere alla cultura* (Palermo: Sellerio, 1980). In this respect the difference with the thought of Bloch is evident.

9. It is probably on this problem (that of the symbolic-iconic sign) that Benjamin's constant interest in Romantic aesthetics and literary criticism is centered. On this problem, see T. Todorov, *Theories of the Symbol*, trans. Catherine Porter (Ithaca, N.Y.: Cornell University Press, 1982). It is against the background of such Romantic theories that one would have to take up the relation between Benjamin's concept of Eros and that of Klages (finally rescued from bad literary "spells," as managed by G. Moretti, *Anima e immagine. Sul "poetico" in Ludwig Klages*, [Palermo: Sellerio, 1985]), which is precisely expressed in the conversation of the soul with the *image*, an image that is not brought forth from the soul, but by which the soul is struck and of which the soul *suffers*, as the image *of* unattainable distance.

10. Here lies one of the most profound affinities between Benjamin and Kafka: for Kafka, in fact, impatience constitutes *the* sin. On this theme, I refer to the second chapter of the first part of my book *Icone*

della Legge (Milan: Adelphi, 1984); a chapter dedicated to Kafka's "questioning."

11. F. Rosenzweig, *Der Stern der Elösung*, pt. 2, p. 210.

* [The Italian word *ritaglio* is semantically richer than its English equivalent; it means both a cutout and a free moment of time, a moment of time that can be spent freely. Therefore the author links *temnein* (to cut) and *tempus* (time), as well as *krinein* (to divide) and *chronos* (time).—Translator's note]

12. See E. Przywara, "Zeit, Raum, Ewigkeit," in *Tempo e eternità* (Padua: CEDAM, 1959); and E. Grassi, "Apocalisse e Storia," in *Apocalisse e Insecuritas* (Milan and Rome, 1954).

13. For a general approach to these themes within the context of the Jewish mystical tradition and its radical discussion in Benjamin (and, in other respects, also in Kafka) the following are fundamental: G. Scholem, *Kabbalah* (New York: Quadrangle, 1974); and G. Scholem, *Zum Verständnis der messianischen Idee im Judentum*, in *Judaica I* (Frankfurt: Suhrkamp, 1977).

* [The author coins the terms "*'stato-' e crono-latria.*" The former means an idolatry of what has been, of what is taken to be a "completed state" (and the author plays on the political, as well as the temporal, senses of the term). The latter refers to an idolatry of chronological time.—Translator's note]

14. On the problem of the "nonchronolatric" conception of time, I refer to my essays collected in *Zeit ohne Kronos*, (Klagenfurt, 1986), and to my article "Chronos e Aion," *Il Centauro* 17 (1986).

Chapter 4. Zodiacs

1. A whole chapter could be devoted to the figure of the angel in Valéry: the entirety of the *Cahiers* is testimony to its importance. More than once, Valéry remarks that Degas was in the habit of calling him an angel!

2. Rabbinical Judaism has always fought openly against the mystical conception of the Chariot, yet without being able to halt its development. In the writings of Qumran this conception already appears central. It is perhaps not useless to quote this passage from the *L'holocauste de Sabbat* ["Songs of the Sabbath Sacrifice"](4Q SL40): "Above the firmament, the Cherubim bless the image of the Throne-Chariot, they acclaim

the majesty of the firmament of light below the seat of its glory." *Les Textes de Qumran*, French trans. by J. Carmagnac, E. Cothenet, and H. Lignée (Paris, 1963). On the extraordinary familiarity of the inhabitants of Qumran with the Angels, see the splendid edition of the manuscripts of Qumran by L. Moraldi (Turin, 1986).

3. The vision of Daniel 7:2 moves from the figure of animals to that of the Son of Man, who is granted sovereignty, glory, and kingdom by the "one of great age." The heavenly being has a *human* appearance.

4. De Lubac (*Exégèse médiévale*, p. 639) analyses the interpretation of Ezekiel given by St. Gregory. The faces and the wings of the four living creatures symbolize the different ways of reading the Scripture. "Per faciem" ("by the face") is expressed the "notitia" (clear and distinct knowledge); "per pennas" ("by the wings") is expressed, instead, the "volatus" (no longer intellectual representation, but spiritual, anagogical movement). As has been already remarked, the "volatus" is essentially free: "ad contemplativae vitae *libertatem* transit" ("it passes to the freedom of contemplative life"). De Lubac, though, rightly insists on the non-contradictory difference between "notitia" and "volatus": if the flight of anagogy transcends the intellectual knowledge of the Scriptures, the obligatory starting point is still represented by the latter (p. 637). The anagogy *completes* the interpretation of the Scriptures by bringing it back to its eschatological *heart*, without effecting any disassociation from the arduously acquired "notitia." The same is true of Dante in the passage quoted previously, who dilates and "universalizes" the theme into the relation between profane religion and Revelation ("The temporal fire and the eternal you have seen, my son, and are come to a part where I myself discern no farther onward," *Purgatorio*, XXVII, 127–129).

5. C. G. Jung, "The Philosophical Tree," in *Alchemical Studies*, Collected Works, vol. 13. (Princeton, N.J.: Princeton University Press, 1967), pp. 279–283.

6. F. Cumont, "Les Anges du paganisme," *Revue d'Histoire des Religions* 72 (1915).

7. E. Bischoff, *Babylonisch-Astrales im Weltbilde des Talmud und Midrash* (Leipzig, 1907).

8. Angelology would thus serve as the fundamental confirmation of that *living* relation between paganism and Revelation of which speak, from nearly opposite points of view, both Schelling in *The Philosophy of Revelation* and Rosenzweig in *The Star of Redemption*. For Schelling's

interpretation of paganism, see X. Tilliette, *La mythologie comprise* (Naples, 1984).

9. *Kāribu* means etymologically "the prayer, that which prays." It is essentially a protecting demon, whose absence exposes man and his temple to the assault of evil powers. But also the "man in white with a scribe's ink horn in his belt" (Ezekiel 9:2) evokes the image of the Babylonian Nabu. The Talmud was well aware of these dangerous "affinities." Rabbi Simeon ben Lakish (third century Palestinian talmudist) put it this way: "The names of the Angels have come with those that returned from Babylon" (quoted in A. Caquot, "Anges et démons en Israel," in *Génies, anges et démons*, p. 133). One should not forget that Babylon, home of prostitution and other earthly abominations, constitutes the absolute negation of Jerusalem. On Babylonian angelology, see B. Teyssèdre, *Anges, astres et cieux. Figures de la destinée et du salut*, ed. Albin Michel (Paris, 1986).

10. C. G. Jung, *Answer to Job* (London: Routledge, 1955).

11. W. Hübner, *Zodiacus Christianus. Jüdisch-christliche Adaptationen des Tierkreises von der Antike bis zur Gegenwart* (Meisenheim, 1983), pp. 37–39.

12. On the imaginary of Hell in the ancient world and the traditions examined here, see P. Xella, *Archeologia dell'inferno* (Verona, 1987).

13. English translation, Violet MacDermot, trans., *Pistis Sophia* (Leiden: E. J. Brill, 1978).

14. For this part of my work, apart from the classic *Sternglaube und Sterndeutung. Die Geschichte und das Wesen der Astrologie*, by F. Boll, C. Bezold, W. Gundel, 4th ed., ed. W. Gundel (1931), see the extraordinary book by Hugo Winckler, *Die babylonische Geisteskultur* (1907). The investigations of Winckler also had widespread influence beyond the specialized milieux. Some of its themes were recovered by F. C. Rang, one of the German writers most esteemed by Hoffmansthal, Benjamin and Rosenzweig, in his *Historische Psychologie des Karnevals* (1927). Cassirer, in the second volume ("Mythical Thought") of *The Philosophy of Symbolic Forms* (English translation, R. Manheim, trans. [New Haven, Conn.: Yale University Press, 1963]) quotes Winckler numerous times, while criticizing in him a certain "panbabylonism."

15. C. Bezold, *Astronomie, Himmelschau und Astralleben bei den Babyloniern* (Heidelberg, 1911).

16. In accordance with the spirit of Augustinian "aesthetics," whose tradition is wonderfully examined by L. Spitzer, *Classical and Christian Ideas of World Harmony* (Baltimore: Johns Hopkins University Press, 1963).

17. In the *Philosophy of Revelation*, Schelling absolutizes this aspect of the Angel and denies, probably following Origen (*Commentary on Romans*, VII, 4), any form of the will to the Angel. One should remember the motif, mentioned previously, of the demon "on the ropes," prisoner of the golden chain that binds the universe: M. Eliade, "Ropes and Puppets," in *Mephistopheles and the Androgyne* (New York, 1965).

18. H. U. von Balthasar, *Studies in Theological style: Clerical Styles*, in *The Glory of the Lord*, vol. 2 (San Francisco: Ignatius Press, 1984).

19. Nonetheless, in the *Banquet* Dante distinguishes between active and contemplative angels, and the *two* forms of blessedness that derive from them: that of "governing" and that of "speculating" (an idea whose connection with Dante's entire philosophy is easily seen). This complicates and problematizes the relation with the Areopagitic angelology—as it has been noticed, for different reasons, by Balthasar himself (*Studies in Theological Styles: Lay Styles*, in *The Glory of the Lord* [San Francisco: Ignatius Press, 1984]. vol. 3, p. 28). See E. Gilson, *Dante et la philosophie* (Paris, 1972), pp. 140–141.

20. Quoted from the *Commentary* by Silvestro da Ferrara to St. Thomas Aquinas, *Summa contra gentiles*, in C. Journet, "L'aventure des anges," in C. Journet, J. Maritain, and P. de la Trinité, *Le péché de l'Ange* (Paris, 1961), p. 20. The same vision is found in the seventeenth century in Bossuet, *Elévations sur les Mystères*, IV, 3.

21. S. Kierkegaard, *Diario*, ed. C. Fabro (Brescia, 1963), vol. 2, p. 618; English translation, G. M. Andersen, trans., *The Diary of S. Kierkegaard* (New York: Philosophical Library, 1960). In this sense, Kierkegaard's *Works of Love* (Princeton, N.J.: Princeton University Press, 1941) are counter to sin.

22. P. Florenskii, *La colonna e il fondamento della verità*, p. 229. One should refer, in this work, especially to the *Seventh Letter* and *Eighth Letter*, dedicated to the themes of Sin and Hell, respectively. Analogous considerations in the brief but very dense essay by A. K. Coomaraswamy, "Satan and Hell", in *Selected Papers*, vol. 2, pp. 23ff (which is also important for the theme of apokatastasis, developed in the following chapter).

23. J. Maritain, "Le péché de l'Ange," in C. Journet, J. Maritain, and P. de la Trinité, *Le péché de l'Ange* pp. 45–48.

24. C. Journet, "L'aventure des anges," in ibid., p. 32.

25. The relation between the protean image of man and the theological tradition is central in H. de Lubac, *L'alba incompiuta del Rinascimento. Pico della Mirandola* (Milan, 1977).

26. R. Guardini, in his *Der Engel in Dantes Göttlicher Komödie*, (Munich, 1951), insists on the "completely Christian" character of the Angels in Dante, without even perceiving the antinomical character of their figures, for which, on the contrary, we have tried to account in this book.

Chapter 5. Apokatastasis

1. H. U. von Balthasar, *Studies in Theological Styles: Lay Styles*, in *The Glory of the Lord*, vol. 3, p. 84.

2. Ibid., p. 87.

3. The reference is to the eternity of simple duration that Plotinus calls *Aidion* and distinguishes clearly from *Aiōn*. On this subject, I refer to my article, "Chronos e Aion," *Il Centauro*, 17 (1986).

4. H. U. von Balthasar, *Studies in Theological Styles: Lay Styles*, p. 100. Indeed, in his poem dedicated to Dante, Schelling exalts the heroic determination of the Poet in traversing the eternal Door and descending into the abyss, but he "forgets" that it is *not* this abyss, this "heart of the earth," that can be saved in the Light, but precisely only he who traverses it, he who abandons it without pity.

5. H. U. von Balthasar, ibid. The specifically angelological problem, connected to this fundamental theological question, is again amply discussed by Balthasar in *Dramatis Personae: Persons in Christ*, in *Theo-drama: A Theological Dramatic Theory*, vol. 3 (San Francisco: Ignatius Press, 1988).

6. Naturally, one should not forget the *paradox* of John (here as elsewhere; for example, on the theme of the *Eikōn*). In fact, the statement we quoted is opposed by: "in iudicium ego in hunc mundum veni" ("For judgment I came into this world") (John 9:39).

7. See S. Boulgakov, *L'Epouse de l'agneau* ["The Bride of the Lamb"] (Lausanne, 1984), Part 3, *L'Eschatologie*, pp. 300–309, 319, 325ff.

But it cannot be only the Son who waits; one has to think that there is hope in the heart of the Father himself, in the perfectly free mission of the Verbum. See C. Péguy, *Le porche du Mystère de la deuxième vertu* (Paris: Gallimard, 1929).

8. John Scot Eriugena translates *apokatastasis* by *restitutio* (restoration), see *Commentarius in evangelium Iohannis* (III, 6).

9. On the contrary, Luther considers Origen to be the third evil Angel (see his "Preface to the Revelation of St. John" [1530]; English translation, C. M. Jacobs, trans., *Luther's Works*, vol. 35): he who has "corrupted the Scriptures with philosophy and reason, as the Universities have hitherto done among us." These positions suffice to clarify the limits of Luther with respect to the Patristic tradition, his radical difference with the German and Flemish mysticism of the preceding centuries, and the essential reasons for the disappearance of the angelological problematic in the theology of the Reformation.

10. H. de Lubac, in his *Histoire et Esprit. L'intelligence de l'Ecriture d'après Origène* (Paris, 1950), is very attentive to this dimension of the mysterium crucis (mystery of the Cross). Nonetheless, this book, in its "vindication" of the orthodoxy of the Origenian exegesis, is forced to avoid completely the skandalon (stumbling block) of the apokatastasis. Analogous limit in J. Daniélou, *Gospel Message and Hellenistic Culture*, trans. J. A. Barker (Philadelphia: Westminster Press, 1973).

11. On the theme of the apokatastasis, see D. Pazzini, *In Principio era il Logos* (Brescia, 1983). This is one of the most philosophically problematic and rich interpretations of the Origenian exegesis. According to Pazzini, the apokatastasis (not a simple return to the initial state, in accordance with its "cyclical" etymological meaning, but a liberation, an acquisition) is not the prerogative of the Father, but is enclosed in the justice of the Son. It has the character of event, of temporality, and it is the Premise of the intervention of the Father, who will "prove through actions his goodness, filling with benefits those that have been educated in the justice of the Son" (Origen, *Commentarium in Johannem*, I, 35). Note the enormous difference between the idea of apokatastasis in this Christian tradition and the one developed in the Neoplatonic milieu (see Proclus, *Elementa theologiae*, 198–199), where it indicates solely the necessity of the soul, fixed to the circular movement of the universe, to relive the same experiences. Far from assuming a redemptive connotation, here the apokatastasis indicates the condemnation of the soul to the destiny of rebirths. A fundamental recovery of Origenian ideas will occur

in Campanella; see N. Badaloni, *Tommaso Campanella* (Milan, 1965), pp. 183–205.

12. On St. Gregory of Nyssa, see the research of J. Daniélou, in *L'être et le temps chez Grégoire de Nysse* (Leiden, 1970). The conceptions of St. Gregory of Nyssa will be recovered by John Scot Eriugena.

13. Luther's positions on this issue are, once again, diametrically opposed. "It is just as if you owed a debt to your liege lord (Lehensherrn) and could not pay it. There are two ways in which you could rid yourself of the debt: either he would take nothing from you and would tear up the account, or some good man would pay it for you (für dich bezahlete) and give you the means to satisfy the account. It is in this latter way that Christ has made us free from the *Law*" ("Preface to the Epistle of St. Paul to the Romans" [1522] in *Luther's Works*, vol. 35, p. 376).

14. As Origen says in a famous text: "The Savior has come down to earth out of pity for the human race. He has patiently experienced our passions before suffering the cross and deigning to take our flesh. . . . What is this passion, then, that he suffered for us? The passion of love (caritatis). But the Father Himself, God of the universe, full of goodness and mercy and pity, does He not suffer in some way? Or do you ignore that, when He takes care of human affairs, He experiences a human passion? . . . The Father Himself is not unmoved! If one prays to Him, He feels compassion, He suffers a passion of love" (Origen, *Homilies on Ezekiel*, VI, 6). The most violent of oppositions separated these conceptions from the radical Docetism of Christian Gnosis, which perhaps finds its most impressive expression in the *Apocalypse of Peter*. And Tertullian (*Against Praxeas*, 29, 6): "sed quomodo filius passus est, si non compassus est et pater?" ("But how could the Son suffer, if the Father did not also suffer with him?") Clement of Alexandria goes so far as to call *mother* what in the Divine Father submits to death. This is why He suffers with us: "By an act of love the Father turned into a woman" (*Stromata*, VI, 16). How are we not to be reminded of the God who suffers at the cry of the Son on the Cross, of which Kierkegaard speaks, and of Simone Weil when she says: "Everything that I suffer, God suffers"? We can barely evoke the complexity of the problem of God's suffering and of the relation between the Father and the Son *on the Cross* in the Crisis theology of the twentieth century. The most important investigations of K. Barth, of Moltmann, of Jüngel, as well as those of Kasper, all turn on these questions, overcoming any confessional "barrier." On the suffering of God, see the last volume of the *Theo-drama* by Balthasar.

15. P. Bettiolo, in the already cited "Introduction" to the *Discorsi spirituali*, has also called attention to the presence of "that single book, large and with the yellow cover" with which Smerdyakov quickly covers the money that proves his crime: they are, once again, *The Sermons of the Saintly Father Isaac of Nineveh.*

16. F. W. J. Schelling, *Philosophische Untersuchungen über das Wesen der menschlichen Freiheit* [1809]. English translation, J. Gutmann, *Schelling: Of Human Freedom* (Chicago: Open Court, 1936).

17. One finds motifs connected to the idea of apokatastasis also in Schleiermacher, see Karl Barth, *Protestant Theology in the Nineteenth Century* (London, 1972).

18. These conceptions, nonetheless, remain foreign to traditional theology, as shown by J. Meyendorff in his *Byzantine Theology* (New York: Fordham University Press, 1979), who does not even cite the investigations of Boulgakov, Florenskii, Frank, Berdyaev, etc. The book by P. Coda, *Evento pasquale* (Rome, 1984), instead, demonstrates the increasing attention given to these conceptions in a certain ambit of Catholic theology. But it would be mistaken to think that the orthodox tradition follows unanimously the traces of St. Gregory of Nyssa, Isaac of Nineveh, etc.; the conceptions of St. Gregory Palamas, for example, are very close to those of Dante.

19. But also in Jewish mysticism the Last Judgment is often awaited as a liberation from the *krisis*, from separation, and not as its absolute fixation. This is how the theme returns in Rosenzweig, *The Star of Redemption*, p. 238: "The ultimate Judgment, anticipating in all eternity, erases the separation by and after confirming it, and quenches *the fires of hell*" (my emphasis). Analogously, Simone Weil in her *Notebooks*: "Reconcile all things, on earth as in the heavens—the end of hell?" Schelling is once again at the origin of this theme, at least within the context of contemporary theology: all this will be remitted to the Father "when even hell will cease to exist; in this eternity there will occur the regeneration of evil, which we must believe in. Neither sin nor its consequences are eternal." Schelling, *Stuttgarter Vorlesungen* [1810], in *Sämmtliche Werke*, ed. K. F. A. Schelling.

20. G. W. F. Hegel, *Aforismi jenesi* [1803–1806] (Milan, 1981), p. 69.

21. In any case, Boulgakov has written a fundamental book on the Angel, *L'Echelle de Jacob* (Paris, 1929).

22. P. Florenskii, *La colonna e il fondamento della verità*, p. 309.

23. Ibid., pp. 212–213.

24. This problematic is central in Rosenzweig. The fact that it is present in an analogous form in orthodox theology, which we have analyzed, is no doubt a sign of the times. At bottom, our essay has pursued the analysis of this sign.

Chapter 6. Birds of the Soul

1. H. U. von Balthasar, *Theo-drama: A Theological Dramatic Theory* (San Francisco: Ignatius Press, 1988), vol. 3, cit., p. 479. There is a remarkable critique here of K. Barth's angelology (which can be found in *Church dogmatics*, vol. 3, book 3 [New York: Harper and Row, 1962]). This critique should come as no surprise given that Karl Barth's magnum opus contains no section specifically dedicated to eschatology (only the fifth volume, which Barth never wrote, would have been dedicated to redemption and eschatology).

2. "Respicite volatilia caeli" ("Look at the birds of the air") (Matthew 6:26). Thus the image of the "divine bird" (*Purgatory*, II, 38) derives from the Christian tradition. On the comparison between Angel and bird in Roman civilization, see M. M. Davy, *Initiation à la symbolique romance* (Paris: Flammarion, 1977).

3. On the origins of this idea of prayer, see the Syrian texts, interpreted and translated by P. Bettiolo, in *Margaritae. Testi siriaci sulla preghiera* (Venice, 1983); as well as the introductions and notes to the texts of the *Philocalia*, ed. M. B. Artioli and M. F. Lovato (Turin, 1982).

4. Dante, here as elsewhere, follows Pseudo-Dionysius who does not mention the linguistic faculties of the Angels. The problem is more complex in St. Thomas Aquinas, who poses the question of how Angels can reciprocally communicate with each other without having recourse to sensible signs. Egidio Romano, Ockham, John Gerson, on the contrary, will maintain the thesis of a language of Angels. On this polemic and its influence on Scholastic thought, see A. Tabarroni, "Il linguaggio degli Angeli," *Prometeo* 12 (1985).

* [The author wants to bring out the etymology of the term: *infant*, from the Latin *in-fans*, "unable to speak."—Translator's note]

5. See H. Imhof, *Rilkes "Gott." R. M. Rilkes Gottesbild als Spiegelung des Unbewussten* (Heidelberg, 1983), pp. 371ff.

6. F. Marc, letter of April 12, 1915, quoted in *Franz Marc. Dal pensiero alla forma*, ed. J. Nigro Covre (Turin, 1971), p. 16.

7. Every sound ek-sists; and in this *ek-*, the pure provenance, the pure virtuality of the Open *signifies*. On this aspect of our investigation, see C. Sini, *Immagini di verità* (Milan, 1985).

8. F. Marc, *I cento aforismi*, ed. G. Franck (Milan, 1982), p. 79.

9. This aspect of the work of Marc was appropiately emphasized by J. Nigro Covre, in *Franz Marc. Dal pensiero alla forma*, p. 18. In addition, the importance of the figure of St. Francis in Rilke's work, not only for the years of "apprenticeship," is well known. The Franciscan influence is noticeable in many currents of the Central European Geisteskultur at the beginning of the century (one has only to think of the young Lukacs or of Bloch).

10. The concert, dedicated to "the memory of an Angel," for the death of the daughter of Alma Mahler and Gropius, veritable Kindertotenlied by Berg, has been analyzed by T. W. Adorno in *Alban Berg, Master of the Smallest Link* (New York, 1991) and is skillfully performed by Mitropoulos and Szigeti.